TEACHER'S PET PUBLICATIONS

PUZZLE PACK
for
The Watsons Go to Birmingham – 1963

based on the book by
Christopher Paul Curtis

Written by
Mary B. Collins

© 2006 Teacher's Pet Publications
All Rights Reserved

The materials in this packet are copyrighted
by Teacher's Pet Publications, Inc.

These pages may be duplicated by the purchaser
for use in the purchaser's own classroom.

Copying any of these materials and distributing them
for any other purpose is a violation of the copyright laws.

© 2006 Teacher's Pet Publications, Inc.
www.tpet.com

INTRODUCTION
If you already own the LitPlan for this title, this Puzzle Pack will refresh your Unit Resource Materials and Vocabulary Resource Materials sections plus give you additional materials you can substitute into the tests. If you do not already have a complete LitPlan, these pages will give you some supplemental materials to use with your own plan. There are two main groups of materials: one set for unit words (such as characters' names, symbols, places, etc.) and one set for vocabulary words associated with the book.

WORD LIST
There is a word list for both the unit words and the vocabulary words. These lists show you which words are being used in the materials and the clues or definitions being used for those words. You may want to give students a word list with clues/definitions to help them, or you may want students to only have a word list (without clues/definitions) if you want them to work a little harder. Both are available for duplication. The word lists can also be your "calling key" for the bingo games.

FILL IN THE BLANK AND MATCHING
There are 4 each of the fill in the blank and matching worksheets for both the unit and vocabulary words. These pages can be used either as extra worksheets for students or as objective parts of a unit test. They can be done individually if students need extra help or as a whole class activity to review the material covered.

MAGIC SQUARES
The magic squares not only reinforce the material covered but also work on reasoning and math skills. Many teachers have told us that their students really enjoy doing these!

WORD SEARCH PUZZLES
The word search words go in all directions, as indicated on your answer keys. Two of the word search puzzles have the clues listed rather than the words. This makes the puzzle a little more difficult, but it reinforces the material better. Two word search puzzles have words only for students who find the clue puzzles too difficult.

CROSSWORD PUZZLES
Both unit and vocabulary word sections have 4 crossword puzzles.

BINGO CARDS
There are 32 individual bingo cards for the unit words and 32 individual bingo cards for the vocabulary words. You can use your word list as a "call list," calling the words at random and marking them off of your list as you go, or you could use the flash cards by cutting them apart and drawing the words at random from a hat (or box or whatever). To make a better review, you might ask for the definition and spelling of each word as you call it out–or you could call out the definitions and have students tell you the words they need to look for on the puzzle.

JUGGLE LETTERS
The vocabulary juggle letter game is intended to help students learn the spellings of the words. One sheet has the definitions listed on it as an extra help for students who need it or to reinforce the definitions if you choose to do so.

FLASH CARDS
We've included a set of vocabulary flash cards you can duplicate, cut, and fold for your students. Some teachers make a few sets for general use by the class; others make a set for each student. Some teachers duplicate them for each student and have the students cut & fold their own. You can cut out just the words and put them in a hat, have each student pick out one word and write the definition and a sentence for that word. Students then swap words and papers, with the next student adding a sentence of his own under the last one. You can have students swap as many times as you like. Each time the student will read the sentences written prior to his own and then add a sentence. You can cut out the words and definitions separately and play "I Have; Who Has?" Each student in the room draws a word and definition. The first student says, "I have (the name of the word). Who has the definition?" The student with the definition reads it then says, "I have (the name of the vocabulary word she has). Who has the definition?" The round continues until all words and definitions have been given.

Watsons Go To Birmingham--1963

No.	Word	Clue/Definition
1.	ALABAMA	State where Grandma Sands lived
2.	APPALACHIAN	Kenny thought these mountains were scary.
3.	BALD	Byron's head after Mr. Watson's punishment.
4.	BAMBI	Instead the meeting was like King Kong and ___.
5.	BATHROOM	There was one for Coloreds Only in Birmingham.
6.	BEARD	Dad said they were tickling God's ___ as they drove.
7.	BIRMINGHAM	City where Momma originally came from.
8.	BOARDWALK	Momma's song was Under the ___.
9.	BOMB	It was set off in the church.
10.	BROWN	Nickname for the family car: ___ Bomber.
11.	BUPHEAD	Byron's friend; helped with new hair style
12.	BYRON	Older brother who helped Kenny at the end of the story
13.	CARP	Game Byron and Buphead played with Larry: Great ___ Escape
14.	CHURCH	Site of Bombings
15.	CODY	Rufus's brother
16.	COLLIER	They were to stay away from ___'s Landing.
17.	CONK	What Byron had done to his hair
18.	COUCH	Kenny hid behind it every day.
19.	DINOSAURS	Kenny's favorite toys
20.	DOVE	Byron killed and buried it.
21.	DROWNED	One boy at the Landing did this.
22.	FINGERS	Momma said she would burn Byron's.
23.	FLINT	Michigan city where Watsons lived
24.	FLY	Dad whistled this tune: Straighten Up and ___ Right
25.	FOUR	Number of girls killed in the church bombing
26.	GOD	Kenny said Byron was ___ of School.
27.	GODZILLA	Kenny thought the meeting would be like King Kong and ___.
28.	HOSPITAL	Byron called where Kenny went The World Famous Watson Pet ___
29.	ICEBOX	Momma called Michigan a giant ___.
30.	JOEY	Byron & Kenny's little sister; she left the bombed church
31.	JUVENILE	Byron was officially called this since he turned thirteen.
32.	KENNY	Narrator of story
33.	KING	Kenny said Larry was ____ of School.
34.	LARRY	He stole Kenny's gloves: ___ Dunn
35.	LAYERS	Momma made the children dress in ___ of clothes in winter.
36.	LAZY	Kenny was teased because he had a ___ eye.
37.	LIPLESS	Kenny's nickname for Byron: ___ Wonder
38.	LJ	He stole Kenny's dinosaurs: __ Jones
39.	MAGIC	Kenny was waiting for this power to make him feel better.
40.	MATCHES	Byron was caught with these in the bathroom.
41.	MICHIGAN	State where Watson family lived.
42.	MIRROR	Place on car where Byron's lips froze
43.	MITCHELL	Owner of store
44.	NAZIS	Rufus did not mind being these when playing dinosaurs.
45.	NOTEBOOK	Where Momma kept the details of the trip
46.	OVEN	Kenny said Birmingham was like one.
47.	PINE	Pinnacle of Western Civilization: ___ tree
48.	PLYMOUTH	Make of the family car
49.	POOH	Byron's name for the whirlpool: Wool ____.
50.	RECORD	Dad put a ___ player in the car.
51.	ROBERT	Grandma's dear friend: Mr. ___

Watsons Go To Birmingham--1963

No.	Word	Clue/Definition
52.	RUFUS	Kenny's friend picked on by other kids
53.	SANDS	Byron was sent to stay with Grandma ___.
54.	SAVIOR	Kenny thought of Rufus as his own personal _____.
55.	SCARY	Kenny's description of the Appalachian Mountains
56.	SHOE	What Kenny brought out of the church
57.	SQUIRRELS	Rufus and Cody thought the ones in Flint were skinny.
58.	SUMMER	Shortest length of time Byron would be in Alabama
59.	SWEDISH	Byron killed bird with ____ Creme
60.	TALKING	It took a while to get used to the Southern way of ___.
61.	TEETH	Momma did not like to show these when smiling.
62.	TOOTHBRSH	Dad did not keep his with the rest of the family's.
63.	TWIN	Byron said the Wool Pooh was Winnie the Pooh's evil ___.
64.	ULTRA	Record player was a True-Tone AB-700 ___ Glide
65.	WEIRD	Family nickname: ___ Watsons
66.	WELFARE	Byron thought this was the reason for signing for food.
67.	WHIRLPOOL	Kenny got caught in one at the Landing.
68.	WINDOWS	Momma had a list of who sat by these each day.
69.	YAK	Kenny's song: Yakety ___

Copyrighted

Fill In the Blanks 1 Watsons Go To Birmingham--1963

1. Instead the meeting was like King Kong and ___.
2. What Byron had done to his hair
3. Kenny thought these mountains were scary.
4. Kenny was teased because he had a ___ eye.
5. What Kenny brought out of the church
6. Place on car where Byron's lips froze
7. Byron said the Wool Pooh was Winnie the Pooh's evil ___.
8. Michigan city where Watsons lived
9. Dad said they were tickling God's ___ as they drove.
10. Byron killed bird with ____ Creme
11. Momma did not like to show these when smiling.
12. Kenny's description of the Appalachian Mountains
13. He stole Kenny's gloves: ___ Dunn
14. It took a while to get used to the Southern way of ___.
15. Kenny thought of Rufus as his own personal _____.
16. Byron was sent to stay with Grandma ___.
17. Owner of store
18. Byron was officially called this since he turned thirteen.
19. Kenny was waiting for this power to make him feel better.
20. Dad did not keep his with the rest of the family's.
21. Kenny said Byron was ___ of School.
22. Dad put a ___ player in the car.
23. Site of Bombings
24. Where Momma kept the details of the trip

Fill In The Blanks 1 Answer Key Watsons Go To Birmingham--1963

BAMBI	1. Instead the meeting was like King Kong and ___.
CONK	2. What Byron had done to his hair
APPALACHIAN	3. Kenny thought these mountains were scary.
LAZY	4. Kenny was teased because he had a ___ eye.
SHOE	5. What Kenny brought out of the church
MIRROR	6. Place on car where Byron's lips froze
TWIN	7. Byron said the Wool Pooh was Winnie the Pooh's evil ___.
FLINT	8. Michigan city where Watsons lived
BEARD	9. Dad said they were tickling God's ___ as they drove.
SWEDISH	10. Byron killed bird with ____ Creme
TEETH	11. Momma did not like to show these when smiling.
SCARY	12. Kenny's description of the Appalachian Mountains
LARRY	13. He stole Kenny's gloves: ___ Dunn
TALKING	14. It took a while to get used to the Southern way of ___.
SAVIOR	15. Kenny thought of Rufus as his own personal _____.
SANDS	16. Byron was sent to stay with Grandma ___.
MITCHELL	17. Owner of store
JUVENILE	18. Byron was officially called this since he turned thirteen.
MAGIC	19. Kenny was waiting for this power to make him feel better.
TOOTHBRSH	20. Dad did not keep his with the rest of the family's.
GOD	21. Kenny said Byron was ___ of School.
RECORD	22. Dad put a ___ player in the car.
CHURCH	23. Site of Bombings
NOTEBOOK	24. Where Momma kept the details of the trip

Fill In The Blanks 2 Watsons Go To Birmingham--1963

_____ 1. He stole Kenny's gloves: ___ Dunn

_____ 2. Family nickname: ___ Watsons

_____ 3. Kenny got caught in one at the Landing.

_____ 4. Pinnacle of Western Civilization: ___ tree

_____ 5. Momma had a list of who sat by these each day.

_____ 6. Byron was officially called this since he turned thirteen.

_____ 7. Byron's head after Mr. Watson's punishment.

_____ 8. Where Momma kept the details of the trip

_____ 9. Byron killed bird with ____ Creme

_____ 10. Kenny's description of the Appalachian Mountains

_____ 11. Shortest length of time Byron would be in Alabama

_____ 12. Momma said she would burn Byron's.

_____ 13. Site of Bombings

_____ 14. Byron said the Wool Pooh was Winnie the Pooh's evil ___.

_____ 15. What Kenny brought out of the church

_____ 16. Byron was sent to stay with Grandma ___.

_____ 17. Momma did not like to show these when smiling.

_____ 18. What Byron had done to his hair

_____ 19. It took a while to get used to the Southern way of ___.

_____ 20. Momma's song was Under the ___.

_____ 21. Kenny thought the meeting would be like King Kong and ___.

_____ 22. City where Momma originally came from.

_____ 23. State where Grandma Sands lived

_____ 24. One boy at the Landing did this.

Fill In The Blanks 2 Answer Key Watsons Go To Birmingham--1963

LARRY	1. He stole Kenny's gloves: ___ Dunn
WEIRD	2. Family nickname: ___ Watsons
WHIRLPOOL	3. Kenny got caught in one at the Landing.
PINE	4. Pinnacle of Western Civilization: ___ tree
WINDOWS	5. Momma had a list of who sat by these each day.
JUVENILE	6. Byron was officially called this since he turned thirteen.
BALD	7. Byron's head after Mr. Watson's punishment.
NOTEBOOK	8. Where Momma kept the details of the trip
SWEDISH	9. Byron killed bird with ____ Creme
SCARY	10. Kenny's description of the Appalachian Mountains
SUMMER	11. Shortest length of time Byron would be in Alabama
FINGERS	12. Momma said she would burn Byron's.
CHURCH	13. Site of Bombings
TWIN	14. Byron said the Wool Pooh was Winnie the Pooh's evil ___.
SHOE	15. What Kenny brought out of the church
SANDS	16. Byron was sent to stay with Grandma ___.
TEETH	17. Momma did not like to show these when smiling.
CONK	18. What Byron had done to his hair
TALKING	19. It took a while to get used to the Southern way of ___.
BOARDWALK	20. Momma's song was Under the ___.
GODZILLA	21. Kenny thought the meeting would be like King Kong and ___.
BIRMINGHAM	22. City where Momma originally came from.
ALABAMA	23. State where Grandma Sands lived
DROWNED	24. One boy at the Landing did this.

Fill In The Blanks 3 Watsons Go To Birmingham--1963

1. Michigan city where Watsons lived
2. Kenny got caught in one at the Landing.
3. Byron was officially called this since he turned thirteen.
4. Byron said the Wool Pooh was Winnie the Pooh's evil ___.
5. Momma said she would burn Byron's.
6. Where Momma kept the details of the trip
7. Kenny's description of the Appalachian Mountains
8. Rufus's brother
9. Byron's head after Mr. Watson's punishment.
10. Dad did not keep his with the rest of the family's.
11. What Byron had done to his hair
12. Owner of store
13. Grandma's dear friend: Mr. ___
14. Place on car where Byron's lips froze
15. Byron killed and buried it.
16. Byron was caught with these in the bathroom.
17. Nickname for the family car: ___ Bomber.
18. Kenny thought the meeting would be like King Kong and ___.
19. Record player was a True-Tone AB-700 ___ Glide
20. Rufus and Cody thought the ones in Flint were skinny.
21. It took a while to get used to the Southern way of ___.
22. One boy at the Landing did this.
23. Kenny's song: Yakety ___
24. City where Momma originally came from.

Fill In The Blanks 3 Answer Key Watsons Go To Birmingham--1963

FLINT	1. Michigan city where Watsons lived
WHIRLPOOL	2. Kenny got caught in one at the Landing.
JUVENILE	3. Byron was officially called this since he turned thirteen.
TWIN	4. Byron said the Wool Pooh was Winnie the Pooh's evil ___.
FINGERS	5. Momma said she would burn Byron's.
NOTEBOOK	6. Where Momma kept the details of the trip
SCARY	7. Kenny's description of the Appalachian Mountains
CODY	8. Rufus's brother
BALD	9. Byron's head after Mr. Watson's punishment.
TOOTHBRSH	10. Dad did not keep his with the rest of the family's.
CONK	11. What Byron had done to his hair
MITCHELL	12. Owner of store
ROBERT	13. Grandma's dear friend: Mr. ___
MIRROR	14. Place on car where Byron's lips froze
DOVE	15. Byron killed and buried it.
MATCHES	16. Byron was caught with these in the bathroom.
BROWN	17. Nickname for the family car: ___ Bomber.
GODZILLA	18. Kenny thought the meeting would be like King Kong and ___.
ULTRA	19. Record player was a True-Tone AB-700 ___ Glide
SQUIRRELS	20. Rufus and Cody thought the ones in Flint were skinny.
TALKING	21. It took a while to get used to the Southern way of ___.
DROWNED	22. One boy at the Landing did this.
YAK	23. Kenny's song: Yakety ___
BIRMINGHAM	24. City where Momma originally came from.

Fill In The Blanks 4 Watsons Go To Birmingham--1963

_____ 1. Byron's friend; helped with new hair style

_____ 2. He stole Kenny's dinosaurs: ___ Jones

_____ 3. Kenny's nickname for Byron: ___ Wonder

_____ 4. Dad put a ___ player in the car.

_____ 5. What Byron had done to his hair

_____ 6. Momma made the children dress in ___ of clothes in winter.

_____ 7. Dad whistled this tune: Straighten Up and ___ Right

_____ 8. Byron killed bird with ___ Creme

_____ 9. Pinnacle of Western Civilization: ___ tree

_____ 10. Kenny got caught in one at the Landing.

_____ 11. Record player was a True-Tone AB-700 ___ Glide

_____ 12. Momma had a list of who sat by these each day.

_____ 13. Nickname for the family car: ___ Bomber.

_____ 14. It took a while to get used to the Southern way of ___.

_____ 15. Kenny said Byron was ___ of School.

_____ 16. Kenny thought of Rufus as his own personal _____.

_____ 17. Momma did not like to show these when smiling.

_____ 18. Site of Bombings

_____ 19. Momma said she would burn Byron's.

_____ 20. Byron killed and buried it.

_____ 21. Byron thought this was the reason for signing for food.

_____ 22. Byron's head after Mr. Watson's punishment.

_____ 23. Kenny's favorite toys

_____ 24. What Kenny brought out of the church

Fill In The Blanks 4 Answer Key Watsons Go To Birmingham--1963

BUPHEAD	1. Byron's friend; helped with new hair style
LJ	2. He stole Kenny's dinosaurs: ___ Jones
LIPLESS	3. Kenny's nickname for Byron: ___ Wonder
RECORD	4. Dad put a ___ player in the car.
CONK	5. What Byron had done to his hair
LAYERS	6. Momma made the children dress in ___ of clothes in winter.
FLY	7. Dad whistled this tune: Straighten Up and ___ Right
SWEDISH	8. Byron killed bird with ___ Creme
PINE	9. Pinnacle of Western Civilization: ___ tree
WHIRLPOOL	10. Kenny got caught in one at the Landing.
ULTRA	11. Record player was a True-Tone AB-700 ___ Glide
WINDOWS	12. Momma had a list of who sat by these each day.
BROWN	13. Nickname for the family car: ___ Bomber.
TALKING	14. It took a while to get used to the Southern way of ___.
GOD	15. Kenny said Byron was ___ of School.
SAVIOR	16. Kenny thought of Rufus as his own personal ___.
TEETH	17. Momma did not like to show these when smiling.
CHURCH	18. Site of Bombings
FINGERS	19. Momma said she would burn Byron's.
DOVE	20. Byron killed and buried it.
WELFARE	21. Byron thought this was the reason for signing for food.
BALD	22. Byron's head after Mr. Watson's punishment.
DINOSAURS	23. Kenny's favorite toys
SHOE	24. What Kenny brought out of the church

Matching 1 Watsons Go To Birmingham--1963

___ 1. TOOTHBRSH   A. Rufus and Cody thought the ones in Flint were skinny.
___ 2. SQUIRRELS   B. What Kenny brought out of the church
___ 3. SANDS   C. It took a while to get used to the Southern way of ___.
___ 4. PINE   D. Kenny said Birmingham was like one.
___ 5. TWIN   E. Momma's song was Under the ___.
___ 6. LAZY   F. Grandma's dear friend: Mr. ___
___ 7. MICHIGAN   G. Shortest length of time Byron would be in Alabama
___ 8. ROBERT   H. He stole Kenny's dinosaurs: ___ Jones
___ 9. BATHROOM   I. State where Watson family lived.
___10. TALKING   J. There was one for Coloreds Only in Birmingham.
___11. TEETH   K. Kenny was teased because he had a ___ eye.
___12. BOARDWALK   L. Kenny said Byron was ___ of School.
___13. BYRON   M. Narrator of story
___14. SUMMER   N. Pinnacle of Western Civilization: ___ tree
___15. CODY   O. Dad did not keep his with the rest of the family's.
___16. SHOE   P. Byron was officially called this since he turned thirteen.
___17. JUVENILE   Q. Byron said the Wool Pooh was Winnie the Pooh's evil ___.
___18. LJ   R. Momma did not like to show these when smiling.
___19. LARRY   S. Rufus's brother
___20. MATCHES   T. Byron was caught with these in the bathroom.
___21. BEARD   U. Older brother who helped Kenny at the end of the story
___22. NOTEBOOK   V. Where Momma kept the details of the trip
___23. OVEN   W. Dad said they were tickling God's ___ as they drove.
___24. KENNY   X. Byron was sent to stay with Grandma ___.
___25. GOD   Y. He stole Kenny's gloves: ___ Dunn

Matching 1 Answer Key Watsons Go To Birmingham--1963

O - 1.	TOOTHBRSH	A. Rufus and Cody thought the ones in Flint were skinny.
A - 2.	SQUIRRELS	B. What Kenny brought out of the church
X - 3.	SANDS	C. It took a while to get used to the Southern way of ___.
N - 4.	PINE	D. Kenny said Birmingham was like one.
Q - 5.	TWIN	E. Momma's song was Under the ___.
K - 6.	LAZY	F. Grandma's dear friend: Mr. ___
I - 7.	MICHIGAN	G. Shortest length of time Byron would be in Alabama
F - 8.	ROBERT	H. He stole Kenny's dinosaurs: ___ Jones
J - 9.	BATHROOM	I. State where Watson family lived.
C - 10.	TALKING	J. There was one for Coloreds Only in Birmingham.
R - 11.	TEETH	K. Kenny was teased because he had a ___ eye.
E - 12.	BOARDWALK	L. Kenny said Byron was ___ of School.
U - 13.	BYRON	M. Narrator of story
G - 14.	SUMMER	N. Pinnacle of Western Civilization: ___ tree
S - 15.	CODY	O. Dad did not keep his with the rest of the family's.
B - 16.	SHOE	P. Byron was officially called this since he turned thirteen.
P - 17.	JUVENILE	Q. Byron said the Wool Pooh was Winnie the Pooh's evil ___.
H - 18.	LJ	R. Momma did not like to show these when smiling.
Y - 19.	LARRY	S. Rufus's brother
T - 20.	MATCHES	T. Byron was caught with these in the bathroom.
W - 21.	BEARD	U. Older brother who helped Kenny at the end of the story
V - 22.	NOTEBOOK	V. Where Momma kept the details of the trip
D - 23.	OVEN	W. Dad said they were tickling God's ___ as they drove.
M - 24.	KENNY	X. Byron was sent to stay with Grandma ___.
L - 25.	GOD	Y. He stole Kenny's gloves: ___ Dunn

Matching 2 Watsons Go To Birmingham--1963

___ 1. NOTEBOOK   A. Family nickname: ___ Watsons
___ 2. TOOTHBRSH   B. Kenny thought of Rufus as his own personal _____.
___ 3. ICEBOX   C. Number of girls killed in the church bombing
___ 4. WINDOWS   D. One boy at the Landing did this.
___ 5. KING   E. What Byron had done to his hair
___ 6. RUFUS   F. Site of Bombings
___ 7. CONK   G. Dad did not keep his with the rest of the family's.
___ 8. BYRON   H. Byron's name for the whirlpool: Wool ____.
___ 9. WEIRD   I. Pinnacle of Western Civilization: ___ tree
___10. FOUR   J. Older brother who helped Kenny at the end of the story
___11. BROWN   K. Kenny's friend picked on by other kids
___12. DINOSAURS   L. Byron & Kenny's little sister; she left the bombed church
___13. SQUIRRELS   M. Kenny said Larry was ____ of School.
___14. DROWNED   N. Momma called Michigan a giant ___.
___15. BAMBI   O. Momma said she would burn Byron's.
___16. LAZY   P. Kenny was teased because he had a ___ eye.
___17. CARP   Q. Nickname for the family car: ___ Bomber.
___18. JOEY   R. Momma had a list of who sat by these each day.
___19. PINE   S. Kenny's description of the Appalachian Mountains
___20. CHURCH   T. They were to stay away from ___'s Landing.
___21. COLLIER   U. Rufus and Cody thought the ones in Flint were skinny.
___22. FINGERS   V. Instead the meeting was like King Kong and ___.
___23. POOH   W. Where Momma kept the details of the trip
___24. SAVIOR   X. Kenny's favorite toys
___25. SCARY   Y. Game Byron and Buphead played with Larry: Great ___ Escape

Matching 2 Answer Key Watsons Go To Birmingham--1963

W - 1.	NOTEBOOK	A. Family nickname: ___ Watsons
G - 2.	TOOTHBRSH	B. Kenny thought of Rufus as his own personal _____.
N - 3.	ICEBOX	C. Number of girls killed in the church bombing
R - 4.	WINDOWS	D. One boy at the Landing did this.
M - 5.	KING	E. What Byron had done to his hair
K - 6.	RUFUS	F. Site of Bombings
E - 7.	CONK	G. Dad did not keep his with the rest of the family's.
J - 8.	BYRON	H. Byron's name for the whirlpool: Wool ____.
A - 9.	WEIRD	I. Pinnacle of Western Civilization: ___ tree
C - 10.	FOUR	J. Older brother who helped Kenny at the end of the story
Q - 11.	BROWN	K. Kenny's friend picked on by other kids
X - 12.	DINOSAURS	L. Byron & Kenny's little sister; she left the bombed church
U - 13.	SQUIRRELS	M. Kenny said Larry was ____ of School.
D - 14.	DROWNED	N. Momma called Michigan a giant ___.
V - 15.	BAMBI	O. Momma said she would burn Byron's.
P - 16.	LAZY	P. Kenny was teased because he had a ___ eye.
Y - 17.	CARP	Q. Nickname for the family car: ___ Bomber.
L - 18.	JOEY	R. Momma had a list of who sat by these each day.
I - 19.	PINE	S. Kenny's description of the Appalachian Mountains
F - 20.	CHURCH	T. They were to stay away from ___'s Landing.
T - 21.	COLLIER	U. Rufus and Cody thought the ones in Flint were skinny.
O - 22.	FINGERS	V. Instead the meeting was like King Kong and ___.
H - 23.	POOH	W. Where Momma kept the details of the trip
B - 24.	SAVIOR	X. Kenny's favorite toys
S - 25.	SCARY	Y. Game Byron and Buphead played with Larry: Great ___ Escape

Copyrighted

Matching 3 Watsons Go To Birmingham--1963

___ 1. LJ   A. Byron said the Wool Pooh was Winnie the Pooh's evil ___.
___ 2. BATHROOM   B. There was one for Coloreds Only in Birmingham.
___ 3. RECORD   C. He stole Kenny's gloves: ___ Dunn
___ 4. SANDS   D. Byron's head after Mr. Watson's punishment.
___ 5. MITCHELL   E. Kenny's friend picked on by other kids
___ 6. LIPLESS   F. Rufus and Cody thought the ones in Flint were skinny.
___ 7. LARRY   G. Kenny's description of the Appalachian Mountains
___ 8. APPALACHIAN   H. Momma called Michigan a giant ___.
___ 9. FLINT   I. Instead the meeting was like King Kong and ___.
___10. MAGIC   J. Byron's friend; helped with new hair style
___11. FOUR   K. Owner of store
___12. NOTEBOOK   L. Byron was sent to stay with Grandma ___.
___13. SCARY   M. Michigan city where Watsons lived
___14. SQUIRRELS   N. Kenny was teased because he had a ___ eye.
___15. RUFUS   O. Kenny's nickname for Byron: ___ Wonder
___16. BUPHEAD   P. Kenny was waiting for this power to make him feel better.
___17. BALD   Q. Kenny thought these mountains were scary.
___18. LAZY   R. Byron's name for the whirlpool: Wool ____.
___19. GODZILLA   S. Dad put a ___ player in the car.
___20. ULTRA   T. Number of girls killed in the church bombing
___21. ICEBOX   U. He stole Kenny's dinosaurs: __ Jones
___22. POOH   V. Where Momma kept the details of the trip
___23. TWIN   W. Record player was a True-Tone AB-700 ___ Glide
___24. BAMBI   X. Kenny thought the meeting would be like King Kong and ___.
___25. BOARDWALK   Y. Momma's song was Under the ___.

Matching 3 Answer Key Watsons Go To Birmingham--1963

U - 1. LJ	A.	Byron said the Wool Pooh was Winnie the Pooh's evil ___.
B - 2. BATHROOM	B.	There was one for Coloreds Only in Birmingham.
S - 3. RECORD	C.	He stole Kenny's gloves: ___ Dunn
L - 4. SANDS	D.	Byron's head after Mr. Watson's punishment.
K - 5. MITCHELL	E.	Kenny's friend picked on by other kids
O - 6. LIPLESS	F.	Rufus and Cody thought the ones in Flint were skinny.
C - 7. LARRY	G.	Kenny's description of the Appalachian Mountains
Q - 8. APPALACHIAN	H.	Momma called Michigan a giant ___.
M - 9. FLINT	I.	Instead the meeting was like King Kong and ___.
P - 10. MAGIC	J.	Byron's friend; helped with new hair style
T - 11. FOUR	K.	Owner of store
V - 12. NOTEBOOK	L.	Byron was sent to stay with Grandma ___.
G - 13. SCARY	M.	Michigan city where Watsons lived
F - 14. SQUIRRELS	N.	Kenny was teased because he had a ___ eye.
E - 15. RUFUS	O.	Kenny's nickname for Byron: ___ Wonder
J - 16. BUPHEAD	P.	Kenny was waiting for this power to make him feel better.
D - 17. BALD	Q.	Kenny thought these mountains were scary.
N - 18. LAZY	R.	Byron's name for the whirlpool: Wool ___.
X - 19. GODZILLA	S.	Dad put a ___ player in the car.
W - 20. ULTRA	T.	Number of girls killed in the church bombing
H - 21. ICEBOX	U.	He stole Kenny's dinosaurs: ___ Jones
R - 22. POOH	V.	Where Momma kept the details of the trip
A - 23. TWIN	W.	Record player was a True-Tone AB-700 ___ Glide
I - 24. BAMBI	X.	Kenny thought the meeting would be like King Kong and ___.
Y - 25. BOARDWALK	Y.	Momma's song was Under the ___.

Matching 4 Watsons Go To Birmingham--1963

___ 1. FLY   A. Record player was a True-Tone AB-700 ___ Glide
___ 2. BEARD   B. Rufus did not mind being these when playing dinosaurs.
___ 3. DOVE   C. Family nickname: ___ Watsons
___ 4. RECORD   D. Momma said she would burn Byron's.
___ 5. YAK   E. What Byron had done to his hair
___ 6. BOMB   F. Byron was sent to stay with Grandma ___.
___ 7. BROWN   G. City where Momma originally came from.
___ 8. BALD   H. Byron was caught with these in the bathroom.
___ 9. COUCH   I. Rufus's brother
___10. MATCHES   J. Momma had a list of who sat by these each day.
___11. WEIRD   K. Momma called Michigan a giant ___.
___12. SUMMER   L. Kenny's favorite toys
___13. SANDS   M. Byron killed and buried it.
___14. ICEBOX   N. Kenny's song: Yakety ___
___15. FINGERS   O. Kenny hid behind it every day.
___16. ULTRA   P. Shortest length of time Byron would be in Alabama
___17. MICHIGAN   Q. State where Watson family lived.
___18. DINOSAURS   R. Kenny thought the meeting would be like King Kong and ___.
___19. BIRMINGHAM   S. Dad said they were tickling God's ___ as they drove.
___20. GODZILLA   T. Dad whistled this tune: Straighten Up and ___ Right
___21. NAZIS   U. Grandma's dear friend: Mr. ___
___22. CONK   V. Byron's head after Mr. Watson's punishment.
___23. WINDOWS   W. It was set off in the church.
___24. ROBERT   X. Nickname for the family car: ___ Bomber.
___25. CODY   Y. Dad put a ___ player in the car.

Matching 4 Answer Key Watsons Go To Birmingham--1963

T - 1. FLY	A.	Record player was a True-Tone AB-700 ___ Glide
S - 2. BEARD	B.	Rufus did not mind being these when playing dinosaurs.
M - 3. DOVE	C.	Family nickname: ___ Watsons
Y - 4. RECORD	D.	Momma said she would burn Byron's.
N - 5. YAK	E.	What Byron had done to his hair
W - 6. BOMB	F.	Byron was sent to stay with Grandma ___.
X - 7. BROWN	G.	City where Momma originally came from.
V - 8. BALD	H.	Byron was caught with these in the bathroom.
O - 9. COUCH	I.	Rufus's brother
H - 10. MATCHES	J.	Momma had a list of who sat by these each day.
C - 11. WEIRD	K.	Momma called Michigan a giant ___.
P - 12. SUMMER	L.	Kenny's favorite toys
F - 13. SANDS	M.	Byron killed and buried it.
K - 14. ICEBOX	N.	Kenny's song: Yakety ___
D - 15. FINGERS	O.	Kenny hid behind it every day.
A - 16. ULTRA	P.	Shortest length of time Byron would be in Alabama
Q - 17. MICHIGAN	Q.	State where Watson family lived.
L - 18. DINOSAURS	R.	Kenny thought the meeting would be like King Kong and ___.
G - 19. BIRMINGHAM	S.	Dad said they were tickling God's ___ as they drove.
R - 20. GODZILLA	T.	Dad whistled this tune: Straighten Up and ___ Right
B - 21. NAZIS	U.	Grandma's dear friend: Mr. ___
E - 22. CONK	V.	Byron's head after Mr. Watson's punishment.
J - 23. WINDOWS	W.	It was set off in the church.
U - 24. ROBERT	X.	Nickname for the family car: ___ Bomber.
I - 25. CODY	Y.	Dad put a ___ player in the car.

Magic Squares 1 Watsons Go To Birmingham--1963

Match the definition with the vocabulary word. Put your answers in the magic squares below. When your answers are correct, all columns and rows will add to the same number.

A. DINOSAURS   E. FOUR   I. LAYERS   M. PLYMOUTH
B. BOARDWALK   F. JOEY   J. SHOE   N. LAZY
C. MAGIC   G. HOSPITAL   K. BIRMINGHAM   O. GODZILLA
D. NAZIS   H. YAK   L. ALABAMA   P. OVEN

1. Byron & Kenny's little sister; she left the bombed church
2. Momma made the children dress in ___ of clothes in winter.
3. Kenny thought the meeting would be like King Kong and ___.
4. Rufus did not mind being these when playing dinosaurs.
5. Make of the family car
6. Momma's song was Under the ___.
7. Kenny's song: Yakety ___
8. City where Momma originally came from.
9. Kenny was waiting for this power to make him feel better.
10. Kenny said Birmingham was like one.
11. What Kenny brought out of the church
12. Number of girls killed in the church bombing
13. State where Grandma Sands lived
14. Byron called where Kenny went The World Famous Watson Pet ___
15. Kenny's favorite toys
16. Kenny was teased because he had a ___ eye.

A=	B=	C=	D=
E=	F=	G=	H=
I=	J=	K=	L=
M=	N=	O=	P=

Magic Squares 1 Answer Key Watsons Go To Birmingham--1963

Match the definition with the vocabulary word. Put your answers in the magic squares below. When your answers are correct, all columns and rows will add to the same number.

A. DINOSAURS
B. BOARDWALK
C. MAGIC
D. NAZIS
E. FOUR
F. JOEY
G. HOSPITAL
H. YAK
I. LAYERS
J. SHOE
K. BIRMINGHAM
L. ALABAMA
M. PLYMOUTH
N. LAZY
O. GODZILLA
P. OVEN

1. Byron & Kenny's little sister; she left the bombed church
2. Momma made the children dress in ___ of clothes in winter.
3. Kenny thought the meeting would be like King Kong and ___.
4. Rufus did not mind being these when playing dinosaurs.
5. Make of the family car
6. Momma's song was Under the ___.
7. Kenny's song: Yakety ___
8. City where Momma originally came from.
9. Kenny was waiting for this power to make him feel better.
10. Kenny said Birmingham was like one.
11. What Kenny brought out of the church
12. Number of girls killed in the church bombing
13. State where Grandma Sands lived
14. Byron called where Kenny went The World Famous Watson Pet ___
15. Kenny's favorite toys
16. Kenny was teased because he had a ___ eye.

A=15	B=6	C=9	D=4
E=12	F=1	G=14	H=7
I=2	J=11	K=8	L=13
M=5	N=16	O=3	P=10

Magic Squares 2 Watsons Go To Birmingham--1963

Match the definition with the vocabulary word. Put your answers in the magic squares below. When your answers are correct, all columns and rows will add to the same number.

A. KING
B. ICEBOX
C. COUCH
D. LIPLESS
E. LAZY
F. PINE
G. TEETH
H. NAZIS
I. GOD
J. JUVENILE
K. OVEN
L. CARP
M. ALABAMA
N. RECORD
O. BUPHEAD
P. FOUR

1. Byron's friend; helped with new hair style
2. Kenny's nickname for Byron: ___ Wonder
3. Byron was officially called this since he turned thirteen.
4. Kenny was teased because he had a ___ eye.
5. Kenny said Byron was ___ of School.
6. Pinnacle of Western Civilization: ___ tree
7. Number of girls killed in the church bombing
8. Kenny hid behind it every day.
9. Rufus did not mind being these when playing dinosaurs.
10. Kenny said Birmingham was like one.
11. Kenny said Larry was ____ of School.
12. Dad put a ___ player in the car.
13. Momma called Michigan a giant ___.
14. State where Grandma Sands lived
15. Momma did not like to show these when smiling.
16. Game Byron and Buphead played with Larry: Great ___ Escape

A=	B=	C=	D=
E=	F=	G=	H=
I=	J=	K=	L=
M=	N=	O=	P=

Magic Squares 2 Answer Key Watsons Go To Birmingham--1963

Match the definition with the vocabulary word. Put your answers in the magic squares below. When your answers are correct, all columns and rows will add to the same number.

A. KING
B. ICEBOX
C. COUCH
D. LIPLESS
E. LAZY
F. PINE
G. TEETH
H. NAZIS
I. GOD
J. JUVENILE
K. OVEN
L. CARP
M. ALABAMA
N. RECORD
O. BUPHEAD
P. FOUR

1. Byron's friend; helped with new hair style
2. Kenny's nickname for Byron: ___ Wonder
3. Byron was officially called this since he turned thirteen.
4. Kenny was teased because he had a ___ eye.
5. Kenny said Byron was ___ of School.
6. Pinnacle of Western Civilization: ___ tree
7. Number of girls killed in the church bombing
8. Kenny hid behind it every day.
9. Rufus did not mind being these when playing dinosaurs.
10. Kenny said Birmingham was like one.
11. Kenny said Larry was ____ of School.
12. Dad put a ___ player in the car.
13. Momma called Michigan a giant ___.
14. State where Grandma Sands lived
15. Momma did not like to show these when smiling.
16. Game Byron and Buphead played with Larry: Great ___ Escape

A=11	B=13	C=8	D=2
E=4	F=6	G=15	H=9
I=5	J=3	K=10	L=16
M=14	N=12	O=1	P=7

Magic Squares 3 Watsons Go To Birmingham--1963

Match the definition with the vocabulary word. Put your answers in the magic squares below. When your answers are correct, all columns and rows will add to the same number.

A. YAK
B. POOH
C. LJ
D. BROWN
E. JUVENILE
F. OVEN
G. WINDOWS
H. ALABAMA
I. GOD
J. BEARD
K. CARP
L. KING
M. BAMBI
N. SQUIRRELS
O. BATHROOM
P. DOVE

1. Kenny's song: Yakety ___
2. Rufus and Cody thought the ones in Flint were skinny.
3. Dad said they were tickling God's ___ as they drove.
4. Byron was officially called this since he turned thirteen.
5. Momma had a list of who sat by these each day.
6. Kenny said Larry was ____ of School.
7. Byron killed and buried it.
8. He stole Kenny's dinosaurs: __ Jones
9. There was one for Coloreds Only in Birmingham.
10. Nickname for the family car: ___ Bomber.
11. State where Grandma Sands lived
12. Game Byron and Buphead played with Larry: Great ___ Escape
13. Kenny said Byron was ___ of School.
14. Kenny said Birmingham was like one.
15. Byron's name for the whirlpool: Wool ____.
16. Instead the meeting was like King Kong and ___.

A=	B=	C=	D=
E=	F=	G=	H=
I=	J=	K=	L=
M=	N=	O=	P=

26
Copyrighted

Magic Squares 3 Answer Key Watsons Go To Birmingham--1963

Match the definition with the vocabulary word. Put your answers in the magic squares below. When your answers are correct, all columns and rows will add to the same number.

A. YAK
B. POOH
C. LJ
D. BROWN
E. JUVENILE
F. OVEN
G. WINDOWS
H. ALABAMA
I. GOD
J. BEARD
K. CARP
L. KING
M. BAMBI
N. SQUIRRELS
O. BATHROOM
P. DOVE

1. Kenny's song: Yakety ___
2. Rufus and Cody thought the ones in Flint were skinny.
3. Dad said they were tickling God's ___ as they drove.
4. Byron was officially called this since he turned thirteen.
5. Momma had a list of who sat by these each day.
6. Kenny said Larry was ____ of School.
7. Byron killed and buried it.
8. He stole Kenny's dinosaurs: __ Jones
9. There was one for Coloreds Only in Birmingham.
10. Nickname for the family car: ___ Bomber.
11. State where Grandma Sands lived
12. Game Byron and Buphead played with Larry: Great ___ Escape
13. Kenny said Byron was ___ of School.
14. Kenny said Birmingham was like one.
15. Byron's name for the whirlpool: Wool ____.
16. Instead the meeting was like King Kong and ___.

A=1	B=15	C=8	D=10
E=4	F=14	G=5	H=11
I=13	J=3	K=12	L=6
M=16	N=2	O=9	P=7

Magic Squares 4 Watsons Go To Birmingham--1963

Match the definition with the vocabulary word. Put your answers in the magic squares below. When your answers are correct, all columns and rows will add to the same number.

A. CODY
B. NAZIS
C. KING
D. BROWN
E. POOH
F. ROBERT
G. LJ
H. SHOE
I. SANDS
J. BATHROOM
K. TALKING
L. WEIRD
M. MITCHELL
N. RUFUS
O. TWIN
P. DINOSAURS

1. What Kenny brought out of the church
2. Rufus's brother
3. Rufus did not mind being these when playing dinosaurs.
4. He stole Kenny's dinosaurs: __ Jones
5. There was one for Coloreds Only in Birmingham.
6. Byron said the Wool Pooh was Winnie the Pooh's evil ___.
7. Kenny's favorite toys
8. Byron was sent to stay with Grandma ___.
9. It took a while to get used to the Southern way of ___.
10. Kenny's friend picked on by other kids
11. Owner of store
12. Family nickname: ___ Watsons
13. Byron's name for the whirlpool: Wool ___.
14. Nickname for the family car: ___ Bomber.
15. Kenny said Larry was ___ of School.
16. Grandma's dear friend: Mr. ___

A=	B=	C=	D=
E=	F=	G=	H=
I=	J=	K=	L=
M=	N=	O=	P=

Magic Squares 4 Answer Key Watsons Go To Birmingham--1963

Match the definition with the vocabulary word. Put your answers in the magic squares below. When your answers are correct, all columns and rows will add to the same number.

A. CODY
B. NAZIS
C. KING
D. BROWN
E. POOH
F. ROBERT
G. LJ
H. SHOE
I. SANDS
J. BATHROOM
K. TALKING
L. WEIRD
M. MITCHELL
N. RUFUS
O. TWIN
P. DINOSAURS

1. What Kenny brought out of the church
2. Rufus's brother
3. Rufus did not mind being these when playing dinosaurs.
4. He stole Kenny's dinosaurs: __ Jones
5. There was one for Coloreds Only in Birmingham.
6. Byron said the Wool Pooh was Winnie the Pooh's evil ___.
7. Kenny's favorite toys
8. Byron was sent to stay with Grandma ___.
9. It took a while to get used to the Southern way of ___.
10. Kenny's friend picked on by other kids
11. Owner of store
12. Family nickname: ___ Watsons
13. Byron's name for the whirlpool: Wool ___.
14. Nickname for the family car: ___ Bomber.
15. Kenny said Larry was ___ of School.
16. Grandma's dear friend: Mr. ___

A=2	B=3	C=15	D=14
E=13	F=16	G=4	H=1
I=8	J=5	K=9	L=12
M=11	N=10	O=6	P=7

Word Search 1 Watsons Go To Birmingham--1963

```
S C D W I W K D F Y R B D P Z N T S W
C O F I B E A R D L H S I D E W S A G
G L I N M C N O L O Y P N V I E U N H
V L N D A G C I A T V N O N B I F D X
P I G O B V S V B J F E S Z U R U S T
S E E W K J S A M X Y Z A L P D R M S
C R R S A I O S O I C O U C H R F I B
A A S R Y C N E B V C J R C E O L T Z
R F T K T B Y G Y F J H S L A C I C D
Y L A Y E R S N T S E N I P D E N H N
U E T B R K O E A A G P M G O R T E G
X W M A S H E B T Z L Q F H A V D L T
N R L T E T L L E E I K S J B N D L L
L J L H H U I S S R D S I Z T Y C B H
G X O R C O N S V R T C U N Y I R R B
H O C O T M E K H L E F P M G W P O B
P S R O A Y V P X B C R O A M J X W N
X Y W M M L U C O N K G M U K E P N B
C A R P J P J X M D E N W O R D R R P
```

Byron & Kenny's little sister; she left the bombed church (4)
Byron killed and buried it. (4)
Byron killed bird with ____ Creme (7)
Byron said the Wool Pooh was Winnie the Pooh's evil ___. (4)
Byron thought this was the reason for signing for food. (7)
Byron was caught with these in the bathroom. (7)
Byron was officially called this since he turned thirteen. (8)
Byron was sent to stay with Grandma ___. (5)
Byron's friend; helped with new hair style (7)
Byron's head after Mr. Watson's punishment. (4)
Byron's name for the whirlpool: Wool ____. (4)
Dad put a ___ player in the car. (6)
Dad said they were tickling God's ___ as they drove. (5)
Dad whistled this tune: Straighten Up and ___ Right (3)
Family nickname: ___ Watsons (5)
Game Byron and Buphead played with Larry: Great ___ Escape (4)
Grandma's dear friend: Mr. ___ (6)
He stole Kenny's dinosaurs: __ Jones (2)
He stole Kenny's gloves: ___ Dunn (5)
Instead the meeting was like King Kong and ___. (5)
It took a while to get used to the Southern way of ___. (7)
It was set off in the church. (4)
Kenny hid behind it every day. (5)
Kenny said Birmingham was like one. (4)
Kenny said Byron was ___ of School. (3)
Kenny said Larry was ____ of School. (4)
Kenny thought of Rufus as his own personal _____. (6)
Kenny was teased because he had a ___ eye. (4)
Kenny was waiting for this power to make him feel better. (5)
Kenny's description of the Appalachian Mountains (5)
Kenny's favorite toys (9)
Kenny's friend picked on by other kids (5)
Kenny's nickname for Byron: ___ Wonder (7)
Kenny's song: Yakety ___ (3)
Make of the family car (8)
Michigan city where Watsons lived (5)
Momma called Michigan a giant ___. (6)
Momma did not like to show these when smiling. (5)
Momma had a list of who sat by these each day. (7)
Momma made the children dress in ___ of clothes in winter. (6)
Momma said she would burn Byron's. (7)
Nickname for the family car: ___ Bomber. (5)
Number of girls killed in the church bombing (4)
Older brother who helped Kenny at the end of the story (5)
One boy at the Landing did this. (7)
Owner of store (8)
Pinnacle of Western Civilization: ___ tree (4)
Record player was a True-Tone AB-700 ___ Glide (5)
Rufus did not mind being these when playing dinosaurs. (5)
Rufus's brother (4)
Shortest length of time Byron would be in Alabama (6)
State where Watson family lived. (8)
There was one for Coloreds Only in Birmingham. (8)
They were to stay away from ___'s Landing. (7)
What Byron had done to his hair (4)
What Kenny brought out of the church (4)

Word Search 1 Answer Key Watsons Go To Birmingham--1963

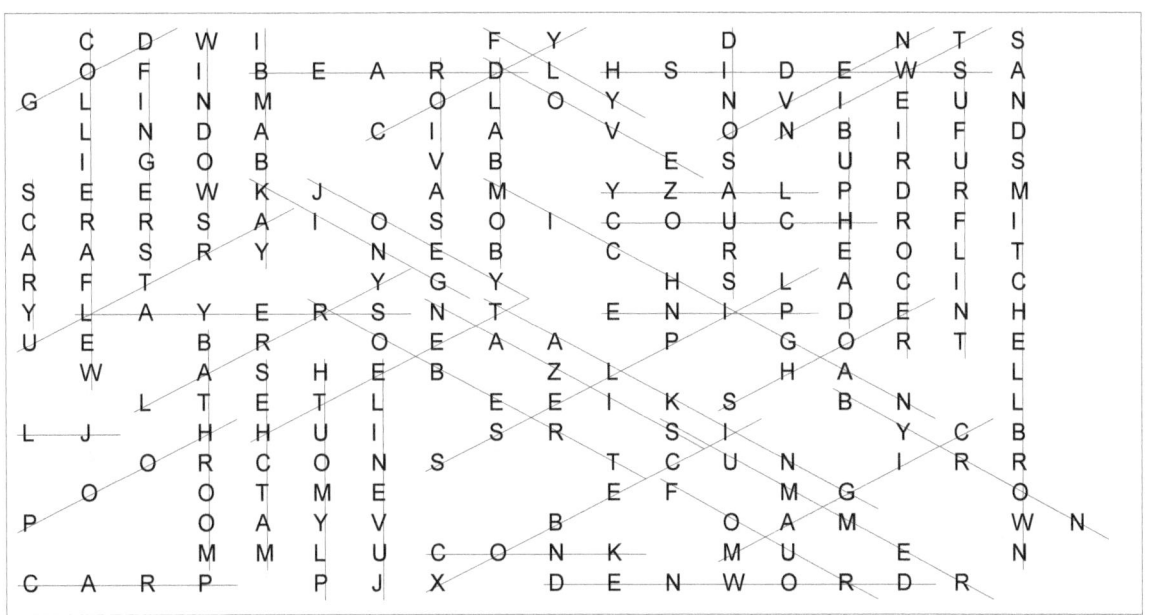

Byron & Kenny's little sister; she left the bombed church (4)
Byron killed and buried it. (4)
Byron killed bird with ____ Creme (7)
Byron said the Wool Pooh was Winnie the Pooh's evil ____. (4)
Byron thought this was the reason for signing for food. (7)
Byron was caught with these in the bathroom. (7)
Byron was officially called this since he turned thirteen. (8)
Byron was sent to stay with Grandma ____. (5)
Byron's friend; helped with new hair style (7)
Byron's head after Mr. Watson's punishment. (4)
Byron's name for the whirlpool: Wool ____. (4)
Dad put a ____ player in the car. (6)
Dad said they were tickling God's ____ as they drove. (5)
Dad whistled this tune: Straighten Up and ____ Right (3)
Family nickname: ____ Watsons (5)
Game Byron and Buphead played with Larry: Great ____ Escape (4)
Grandma's dear friend: Mr. ____ (6)
He stole Kenny's dinosaurs: __ Jones (2)
He stole Kenny's gloves: ____ Dunn (5)
Instead the meeting was like King Kong and ____. (5)
It took a while to get used to the Southern way of ____. (7)
It was set off in the church. (4)
Kenny hid behind it every day. (5)
Kenny said Birmingham was like one. (4)
Kenny said Byron was ____ of School. (3)
Kenny said Larry was ____ of School. (4)
Kenny thought of Rufus as his own personal _____. (6)

Kenny was teased because he had a ____ eye. (4)
Kenny was waiting for this power to make him feel better. (5)
Kenny's description of the Appalachian Mountains (5)
Kenny's favorite toys (9)
Kenny's friend picked on by other kids (5)
Kenny's nickname for Byron: ____ Wonder (7)
Kenny's song: Yakety ____ (3)
Make of the family car (8)
Michigan city where Watsons lived (5)
Momma called Michigan a giant ____. (6)
Momma did not like to show these when smiling. (5)
Momma had a list of who sat by these each day. (7)
Momma made the children dress in ____ of clothes in winter. (6)
Momma said she would burn Byron's. (7)
Nickname for the family car: ____ Bomber. (5)
Number of girls killed in the church bombing (4)
Older brother who helped Kenny at the end of the story (5)
One boy at the Landing did this. (7)
Owner of store (8)
Pinnacle of Western Civilization: ____ tree (4)
Record player was a True-Tone AB-700 ____ Glide (5)
Rufus did not mind being these when playing dinosaurs. (5)
Rufus's brother (4)
Shortest length of time Byron would be in Alabama (6)
State where Watson family lived. (8)
There was one for Coloreds Only in Birmingham. (8)
They were to stay away from ____'s Landing. (7)
What Byron had done to his hair (4)
What Kenny brought out of the church (4)

Word Search 2 Watsons Go To Birmingham--1963

```
T E E T H S D S D S L E R R I U Q S T
B A H N U M S S M Q A R C F D Z W C R
C O L M A E D W A H Y U G Y W E E O O
R V M K L Z L X H K E F S P D L V L B
L E V P I V I J G G R U X I I D A L E
R N I B D N B S N S S S S N C C L I R
X L N B M W G A I M A H E E O R A E T
F B A T H R O O M L B V C B D J B R H
S O G Z V Y K Z R B U W I R Y F A P P
G M I G R T Z J I J I L A O H O M S T
L B H A M D G G B C S E D O R U A N S
J H C X M T O O T H B R S H P R I N R
M S I O B D D V O U X P R O T L I O E
D N M J U U Y E E L I T E O F W W R C
H F F L O C P Y B T V C G P T F E Y O
B A L D F E H H A R C O N K A Y I B R
F C Y A Z J Y L E A O J I Y I R R F D
A L L I Z D O G D A P W F Y C N D Z J
S A N D S Y R R A L D T N Y M A G I C
```

Byron & Kenny's little sister; she left the bombed church (4)
Byron called where Kenny went The World Famous Watson Pet ___ (8)
Byron killed and buried it. (4)
Byron killed bird with ____ Creme (7)
Byron said the Wool Pooh was Winnie the Pooh's evil ___. (4)
Byron was officially called this since he turned thirteen. (8)
Byron was sent to stay with Grandma ___. (5)
Byron's friend; helped with new hair style (7)
Byron's head after Mr. Watson's punishment. (4)
Byron's name for the whirlpool: Wool ____. (4)
City where Momma originally came from. (10)
Dad did not keep his with the rest of the family's. (9)
Dad put a ___ player in the car. (6)
Dad said they were tickling God's ___ as they drove. (5)
Dad whistled this tune: Straighten Up and ___ Right (3)
Family nickname: ___ Watsons (5)
Game Byron and Buphead played with Larry: Great ___ Escape (4)
Grandma's dear friend: Mr. ___ (6)
He stole Kenny's dinosaurs: __ Jones (2)
He stole Kenny's gloves: ___ Dunn (5)
Instead the meeting was like King Kong and ___. (5)
It took a while to get used to the Southern way of ___. (7)
It was set off in the church. (4)
Kenny hid behind it every day. (5)
Kenny said Birmingham was like one. (4)
Kenny said Byron was ___ of School. (3)
Kenny said Larry was ____ of School. (4)

Kenny thought of Rufus as his own personal _____. (6)
Kenny thought the meeting would be like King Kong and ___. (8)
Kenny was teased because he had a ___ eye. (4)
Kenny was waiting for this power to make him feel better. (5)
Kenny's description of the Appalachian Mountains (5)
Kenny's friend picked on by other kids (5)
Kenny's nickname for Byron: ___ Wonder (7)
Kenny's song: Yakety ___ (3)
Michigan city where Watsons lived (5)
Momma did not like to show these when smiling. (5)
Momma made the children dress in ___ of clothes in winter. (6)
Momma said she would burn Byron's. (7)
Nickname for the family car: ___ Bomber. (5)
Number of girls killed in the church bombing (4)
Older brother who helped Kenny at the end of the story (5)
Pinnacle of Western Civilization: ___ tree (4)
Record player was a True-Tone AB-700 ___ Glide (5)
Rufus and Cody thought the ones in Flint were skinny. (9)
Rufus did not mind being these when playing dinosaurs. (5)
Rufus's brother (4)
Shortest length of time Byron would be in Alabama (6)
State where Grandma Sands lived (7)
State where Watson family lived. (8)
There was one for Coloreds Only in Birmingham. (8)
They were to stay away from ___'s Landing. (7)
What Byron had done to his hair (4)
What Kenny brought out of the church (4)

Word Search 2 Answer Key Watsons Go To Birmingham--1963

Byron & Kenny's little sister; she left the bombed church (4)
Byron called where Kenny went The World Famous Watson Pet ___ (8)
Byron killed and buried it. (4)
Byron killed bird with ____ Creme (7)
Byron said the Wool Pooh was Winnie the Pooh's evil ___. (4)
Byron was officially called this since he turned thirteen. (8)
Byron was sent to stay with Grandma ___. (5)
Byron's friend; helped with new hair style (7)
Byron's head after Mr. Watson's punishment. (4)
Byron's name for the whirlpool: Wool ____. (4)
City where Momma originally came from. (10)
Dad did not keep his with the rest of the family's. (9)
Dad put a ___ player in the car. (6)
Dad said they were tickling God's ___ as they drove. (5)
Dad whistled this tune: Straighten Up and ___ Right (3)
Family nickname: ___ Watsons (5)
Game Byron and Buphead played with Larry: Great ___ Escape (4)
Grandma's dear friend: Mr. ___ (6)
He stole Kenny's dinosaurs: __ Jones (2)
He stole Kenny's gloves: ___ Dunn (5)
Instead the meeting was like King Kong and ___. (5)
It took a while to get used to the Southern way of ___. (7)
It was set off in the church. (4)
Kenny hid behind it every day. (5)
Kenny said Birmingham was like one. (4)
Kenny said Byron was ___ of School. (3)
Kenny said Larry was ____ of School. (4)

Kenny thought of Rufus as his own personal _____. (6)
Kenny thought the meeting would be like King Kong and ___. (8)
Kenny was teased because he had a ___ eye. (4)
Kenny was waiting for this power to make him feel better. (5)
Kenny's description of the Appalachian Mountains (5)
Kenny's friend picked on by other kids (5)
Kenny's nickname for Byron: ___ Wonder (7)
Kenny's song: Yakety ___ (3)
Michigan city where Watsons lived (5)
Momma did not like to show these when smiling. (5)
Momma made the children dress in ___ of clothes in winter. (6)
Momma said she would burn Byron's. (7)
Nickname for the family car: ___ Bomber. (5)
Number of girls killed in the church bombing (4)
Older brother who helped Kenny at the end of the story (5)
Pinnacle of Western Civilization: ___ tree (4)
Record player was a True-Tone AB-700 ___ Glide (5)
Rufus and Cody thought the ones in Flint were skinny. (9)
Rufus did not mind being these when playing dinosaurs. (5)
Rufus's brother (4)
Shortest length of time Byron would be in Alabama (6)
State where Grandma Sands lived (7)
State where Watson family lived. (8)
There was one for Coloreds Only in Birmingham. (8)
They were to stay away from ___'s Landing. (7)
What Byron had done to his hair (4)
What Kenny brought out of the church (4)

Word Search 3 Watsons Go To Birmingham--1963

```
G J L F L I N T H A M A B A L A Z T C D
B R U I L A Y E R S I Z A L L I Z D O G
D N S V P T W I N S C E R A F L E W U F
I H V U E L T V Z F H S P T I R K N C Y
N J P G M N E L S G I Z Y I B D G E H D
O H P N K M I S Y C G N G P M O C V R D
S Q U I R R E L S S A N D S A V I O R C
A P N K N D F R E Z N R E O B E C A N R
U G O L P E E U I G S H Y H R E E C L K
R F R A W G V S L M C G H L R B C P A S
S B Y T N W S J Y T O O T H B R S H R H
G H B I N U Y W A M R P E T C L D V R Z
M O F W F B P M E Q R A E U D A J B Y N
I T D U P O O H G D V Y T O Z Z G J Y Y
T R R R I M N Y J S I W L M B Y L E A M
C X W O C B R Q M F E S N Y G A O Q K B
H L C B E G M A G I C S H L F J L Z G F
E J A E B F O U R D A E H P U B Y D O C
L W R R O R Q D N O T E B O O K L K Y Z
L S P T X W H I R L P O O L E B R O W N
```

ALABAMA	DINOSAURS	KING	OVEN	SUMMER
BALD	DOVE	LARRY	PINE	SWEDISH
BAMBI	FINGERS	LAYERS	PLYMOUTH	TALKING
BEARD	FLINT	LAZY	POOH	TEETH
BOMB	FLY	LIPLESS	RECORD	TOOTHBRSH
BROWN	FOUR	LJ	ROBERT	TWIN
BUPHEAD	GOD	MAGIC	RUFUS	ULTRA
BYRON	GODZILLA	MATCHES	SANDS	WEIRD
CARP	HOSPITAL	MICHIGAN	SAVIOR	WELFARE
CODY	ICEBOX	MITCHELL	SCARY	WHIRLPOOL
CONK	JOEY	NAZIS	SHOE	YAK
COUCH	JUVENILE	NOTEBOOK	SQUIRRELS	

Word Search 3 Answer Key Watsons Go To Birmingham--1963

```
      J  L  F  L  I  N  T     A  M  A  B  A  L  A        C
         U  I  L  A  Y  E  R  S  I     A  L  L  I  Z  D  O  G
   D     S  V  P  T  W  I  N     C  E  R  A  F  L  E  W     U
   I        U  E  L           H           T  I           N     C
   N        G  M  N  E        S           I  B  D        E     H  D
   O     P  N  K  M  I  S  Y  C  G  N     P  M  O  C  V  R     D
   S  Q  U  I  R  R  E  L  S  S  A  N  D  S  A  V  I  O  R
   A     N  K  N     F  R  E  Z  N  R  E  O  B  E  C  A     N
   U     G  O  L     E  E  U  I        H  Y  H     E  E     L  K
   R     R  A        G     S  L     C     H     R  B        A
   S     Y  T     N     S           T  O  O  T  H  B  R  S  H  R
   G     B  I        U     W        R     E  T     L           R
   M  O  F        F  B     M  E        A  E  U     A           Y
   I        D  U  P  O  O  H     D        T  O     Z           Y
   T        R  R  I  M                 I  W     M  B        E  A
   C           O  C  B              E  S     Y     A  O        K
   H        C  B  E     M  A  G  I  C  S  H  L     J  L
   E     J  A  E  B  F  O  U  R  D  A  E  H  P  U  B  Y  D  O  C
   L        R  R  O           D  N  O  T  E  B  O  O  K
   L        P  T  X  W  H  I  R  L  P  O  O  L  E  B  R  O  W  N
```

ALABAMA	DINOSAURS	KING	OVEN	SUMMER
BALD	DOVE	LARRY	PINE	SWEDISH
BAMBI	FINGERS	LAYERS	PLYMOUTH	TALKING
BEARD	FLINT	LAZY	POOH	TEETH
BOMB	FLY	LIPLESS	RECORD	TOOTHBRSH
BROWN	FOUR	LJ	ROBERT	TWIN
BUPHEAD	GOD	MAGIC	RUFUS	ULTRA
BYRON	GODZILLA	MATCHES	SANDS	WEIRD
CARP	HOSPITAL	MICHIGAN	SAVIOR	WELFARE
CODY	ICEBOX	MITCHELL	SCARY	WHIRLPOOL
CONK	JOEY	NAZIS	SHOE	YAK
COUCH	JUVENILE	NOTEBOOK	SQUIRRELS	

Word Search 4 Watsons Go To Birmingham--1963

```
S W O D N I W C S R U A S O N I D S S H
R Q W L Y B M U A T Z B R A C M N U W M
F H U E M X F Q J R W Q R E N A J M E Q
S P O I Y U Z X L C P I B E Z D S M D H
X H K S R B Y R O N J O N I C R S E I K
S B I S P R K T B Y X C S B Z O T R S C
P O N B J I E Z E Y W O H M N B R J H D
R A G N D R T L K E W U H A R E J D O D
S R E G N I F A S E T C I B X R D O V F
C D P U F H B J L Y S H P M A T C H E S
D W Z D L N Q F T Z C A R X O X Z N N Y
Z A G F J T A F X A T E V O B W I Y B N
Y L Y F L R R P L C I J T I M P E C M H
F K W A E Y D A O L B H B R O W N I G Y
B F R Z K A P N L O B A G K B R T G R R
N R D J E P K O S R H R L R D C Y A Z D
Y Q W H A S C K S B D F R D H R O M B S
L I P L E S S H G O D U B E A R D D C P
J U V E N I L E V S O Q L C L A Z Y Y C
B F L I N T M E T F K L S R E Y A L Z F
```

APPALACHIAN	CONK	JUVENILE	PINE	TEETH
BALD	COUCH	KING	POOH	TOOTHBRSH
BAMBI	DINOSAURS	LARRY	RECORD	TWIN
BEARD	DOVE	LAYERS	ROBERT	ULTRA
BOARDWALK	FINGERS	LAZY	RUFUS	WEIRD
BOMB	FLINT	LIPLESS	SANDS	WELFARE
BROWN	FLY	LJ	SAVIOR	WINDOWS
BUPHEAD	FOUR	MAGIC	SCARY	YAK
BYRON	GOD	MATCHES	SHOE	
CARP	HOSPITAL	MITCHELL	SQUIRRELS	
CODY	ICEBOX	NAZIS	SUMMER	
COLLIER	JOEY	OVEN	SWEDISH	

Word Search 4 Answer Key Watsons Go To Birmingham--1963

```
S W O D N I W C S R U A S O N I D S S
  Q           U A T       A C   N U W
  H U E     F   R W   R E N A   M M E
    O I   U       P I B E Z D   M   D
  H K S R B Y R O N   O N I C R S E I
S B I   P R   T     X C S B   O   R S
  O N   I E   E       O   M N B R   H
  A G     T L   E W U   A   E J D O V
S R E G N I F A S E T C I B   R   O   
  D   U     J L   S H   M A T C H E S
  W           F   C A R   O     N   Y
  A   F   T A     A   E V O B W I
  L Y   L R R P L C I   T   M P E C M
  K   A E Y D A O L B H B R O W N I
    R   K A P N L O B A   B R T G   R
    R   E P K O   R H   L   C Y A   D
Y       H A   C   S   D   R D H R O M
L I P L E S S H G O D U B E A R D D
J U V E N I L E V   O   L C L A Z Y Y
B F L I N T   E   F   L S R E Y A L
```

APPALACHIAN	CONK	JUVENILE	PINE	TEETH
BALD	COUCH	KING	POOH	TOOTHBRSH
BAMBI	DINOSAURS	LARRY	RECORD	TWIN
BEARD	DOVE	LAYERS	ROBERT	ULTRA
BOARDWALK	FINGERS	LAZY	RUFUS	WEIRD
BOMB	FLINT	LIPLESS	SANDS	WELFARE
BROWN	FLY	LJ	SAVIOR	WINDOWS
BUPHEAD	FOUR	MAGIC	SCARY	YAK
BYRON	GOD	MATCHES	SHOE	
CARP	HOSPITAL	MITCHELL	SQUIRRELS	
CODY	ICEBOX	NAZIS	SUMMER	
COLLIER	JOEY	OVEN	SWEDISH	

Crossword 1 Watsons Go To Birmingham--1963

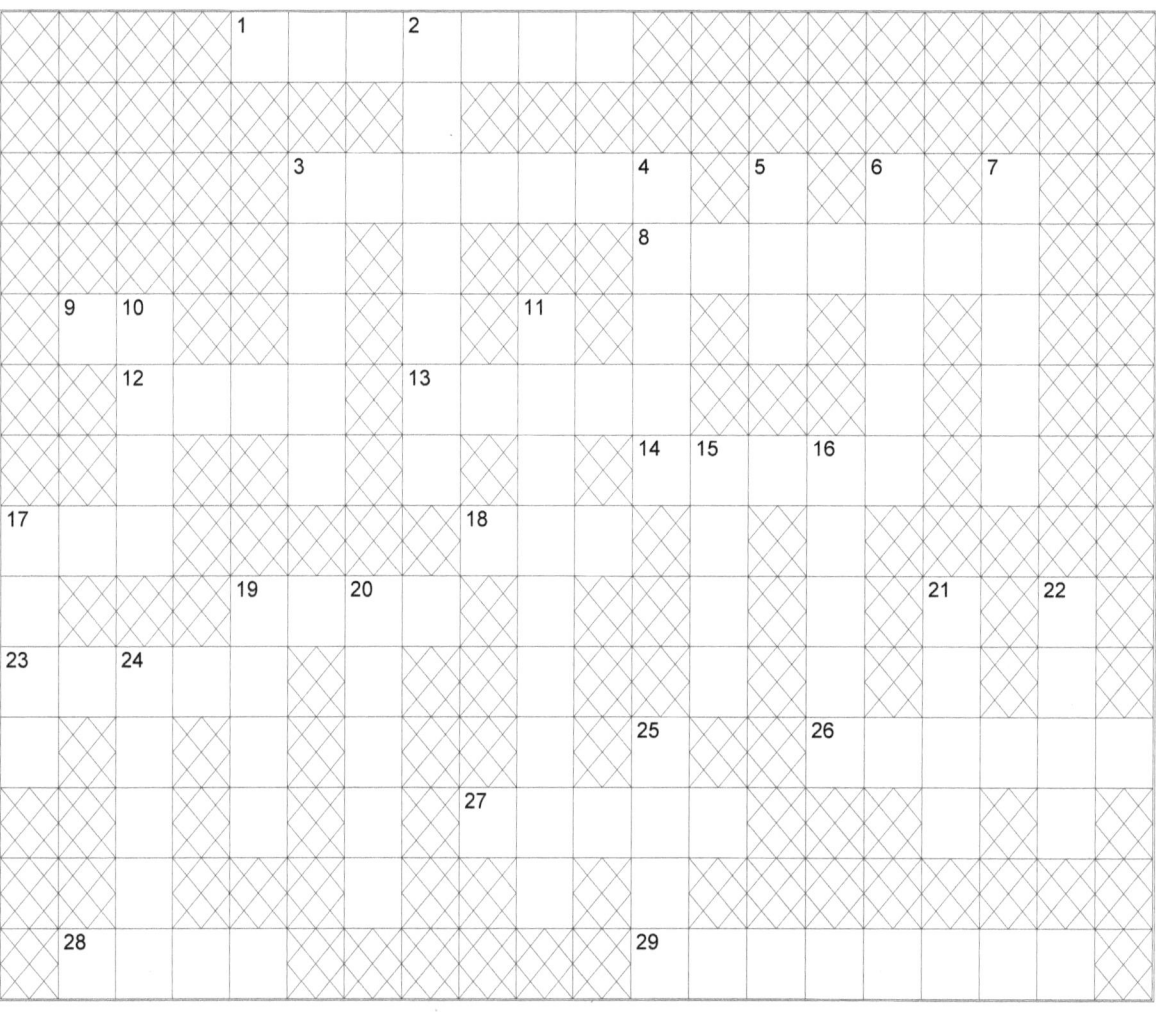

Across
1. One boy at the Landing did this.
3. Momma said she would burn Byron's.
8. State where Grandma Sands lived
9. He stole Kenny's dinosaurs: __ Jones
12. Kenny said Birmingham was like one.
13. Family nickname: ___ Watsons
14. Kenny's description of the Appalachian Mountains
17. Dad whistled this tune: Straighten Up and ___ Right
18. Kenny said Byron was ___ of School.
19. It was set off in the church.
23. Record player was a True-Tone AB-700 ___ Glide
26. Kenny thought of Rufus as his own personal _____.
27. Nickname for the family car: ___ Bomber.
28. What Kenny brought out of the church
29. Where Momma kept the details of the trip

Down
2. Momma had a list of who sat by these each day.
3. Michigan city where Watsons lived
4. Byron was sent to stay with Grandma ___.
5. Kenny's song: Yakety ___
6. He stole Kenny's gloves: ___ Dunn
7. Instead the meeting was like King Kong and ___.
10. Byron & Kenny's little sister; she left the bombed church
11. Kenny's favorite toys
15. Game Byron and Buphead played with Larry: Great ___ Escape
16. Kenny's friend picked on by other kids
17. Number of girls killed in the church bombing
19. Byron's head after Mr. Watson's punishment.
20. Kenny was waiting for this power to make him feel better.
21. Byron killed and buried it.
22. Byron's name for the whirlpool: Wool ____.
24. Momma did not like to show these when smiling.
25. Byron said the Wool Pooh was Winnie the Pooh's evil ___.

Crossword 1 Answer Key Watsons Go To Birmingham--1963

			¹D	R	O	²W	N	E	D						
						I									
			³F	I	N	G	E	R	⁴S		⁵Y		⁶L		⁷B
			L			D			⁸A	L	A	B	A	M	A
⁹L	¹⁰J		I			¹¹O			N		K		R		M
	¹²O	V	E	N		¹³W	E	I	R	D			R		B
	E			T		S			¹⁴S	¹⁵C	A	¹⁶R	Y		I
¹⁷F	L	Y				¹⁸G	O	D		A		U			
O			¹⁹B	²⁰O	M	B				A		F		²¹D		²²P
²³U	²⁴L	T	R	A		A				P		U		O		O
R	E		L		G			A		²⁵T		²⁶S	A	V	I	O	R
	E		D		I		²⁷B	R	O	W	N			E		H
	T				C		S			I					
	²⁸S	H	O	E						²⁹N	O	T	E	B	O	O	K

Across
1. One boy at the Landing did this.
3. Momma said she would burn Byron's.
8. State where Grandma Sands lived
9. He stole Kenny's dinosaurs: __ Jones
12. Kenny said Birmingham was like one.
13. Family nickname: ___ Watsons
14. Kenny's description of the Appalachian Mountains
17. Dad whistled this tune: Straighten Up and ___ Right
18. Kenny said Byron was ___ of School.
19. It was set off in the church.
23. Record player was a True-Tone AB-700 ___ Glide
26. Kenny thought of Rufus as his own personal _____.
27. Nickname for the family car: ___ Bomber.
28. What Kenny brought out of the church
29. Where Momma kept the details of the trip

Down
2. Momma had a list of who sat by these each day.
3. Michigan city where Watsons lived
4. Byron was sent to stay with Grandma ___.
5. Kenny's song: Yakety ___
6. He stole Kenny's gloves: ___ Dunn
7. Instead the meeting was like King Kong and ___.
10. Byron & Kenny's little sister; she left the bombed church
11. Kenny's favorite toys
15. Game Byron and Buphead played with Larry: Great ___ Escape
16. Kenny's friend picked on by other kids
17. Number of girls killed in the church bombing
19. Byron's head after Mr. Watson's punishment.
20. Kenny was waiting for this power to make him feel better.
21. Byron killed and buried it.
22. Byron's name for the whirlpool: Wool ____.
24. Momma did not like to show these when smiling.
25. Byron said the Wool Pooh was Winnie the Pooh's evil ___.

Crossword 2 Watsons Go To Birmingham--1963

Across
1. Byron's head after Mr. Watson's punishment.
5. Byron killed and buried it.
6. There was one for Coloreds Only in Birmingham.
10. Momma called Michigan a giant ___.
11. He stole Kenny's dinosaurs: __ Jones
12. Kenny's song: Yakety ___
14. Game Byron and Buphead played with Larry: Great ___ Escape
15. Byron was sent to stay with Grandma ___.
17. Byron said the Wool Pooh was Winnie the Pooh's evil ___.
19. Momma said she would burn Byron's.
21. Rufus's brother
22. Kenny's friend picked on by other kids
23. Byron's name for the whirlpool: Wool ____.

Down
1. Dad said they were tickling God's ___ as they drove.
2. Kenny's nickname for Byron: ___ Wonder
3. What Kenny brought out of the church
4. They were to stay away from ___'s Landing.
5. One boy at the Landing did this.
7. State where Grandma Sands lived
8. State where Watson family lived.
9. Byron thought this was the reason for signing for food.
13. He stole Kenny's gloves: ___ Dunn
14. Kenny hid behind it every day.
16. Kenny thought of Rufus as his own personal _____.
18. Family nickname: ___ Watsons
19. Number of girls killed in the church bombing
20. Kenny said Byron was ___ of School.

Crossword 2 Answer Key Watsons Go To Birmingham--1963

										1 B	2 L	D
		3 S		4 C				5 D	O	V	E	I
6 B	7 A	T	H	R	O	O	M		9 W	R	A	P
	L		O		L		10 I	C	E	B	O	X		R	11 L	J
	A		E		L		C		L		W		D	E	
	B				I		C	H		F		W			S	
12 Y	A	K			E		I		A		E			S	
	M				R		G		R		D		13 L		
14 C	A	R	P			A			E		15 S	A	N	D	16 S
O				17 T	18 W	I	N						R		A
U					E			19 F	I	N	20 G	E	R	S	V
21 C	O	D	Y		I			O			O		Y		I
H					22 R	U	F	U	S		D		23 P	O	O	H
					D			R							R

Across
1. Byron's head after Mr. Watson's punishment.
5. Byron killed and buried it.
6. There was one for Coloreds Only in Birmingham.
10. Momma called Michigan a giant ___.
11. He stole Kenny's dinosaurs: __ Jones
12. Kenny's song: Yakety ___
14. Game Byron and Buphead played with Larry: Great ___ Escape
15. Byron was sent to stay with Grandma ___.
17. Byron said the Wool Pooh was Winnie the Pooh's evil ___.
19. Momma said she would burn Byron's.
21. Rufus's brother
22. Kenny's friend picked on by other kids
23. Byron's name for the whirlpool: Wool ____.

Down
1. Dad said they were tickling God's ___ as they drove.
2. Kenny's nickname for Byron: ___ Wonder
3. What Kenny brought out of the church
4. They were to stay away from ___'s Landing.
5. One boy at the Landing did this.
7. State where Grandma Sands lived
8. State where Watson family lived.
9. Byron thought this was the reason for signing for food.
13. He stole Kenny's gloves: ___ Dunn
14. Kenny hid behind it every day.
16. Kenny thought of Rufus as his own personal _____.
18. Family nickname: ___ Watsons
19. Number of girls killed in the church bombing
20. Kenny said Byron was ___ of School.

Crossword 3 Watsons Go To Birmingham--1963

Across

1. Rufus and Cody thought the ones in Flint were skinny.
7. Dad said they were tickling God's ___ as they drove.
10. Kenny said Birmingham was like one.
11. Dad put a ___ player in the car.
14. Number of girls killed in the church bombing
15. Kenny said Larry was ___ of School.
17. Rufus did not mind being these when playing dinosaurs.
19. Pinnacle of Western Civilization: ___ tree
20. Game Byron and Buphead played with Larry: Great ___ Escape
22. Kenny said Byron was ___ of School.
23. Older brother who helped Kenny at the end of the story
24. Where Momma kept the details of the trip

Down

1. Byron killed bird with ____ Creme
2. Record player was a True-Tone AB-700 ___ Glide
3. Grandma's dear friend: Mr. ___
4. He stole Kenny's dinosaurs: __ Jones
5. Kenny's song: Yakety ___
6. State where Watson family lived.
7. City where Momma originally came from.
8. Byron killed and buried it.
9. Byron thought this was the reason for signing for food.
12. Shortest length of time Byron would be in Alabama
13. Kenny was teased because he had a ___ eye.
16. Momma called Michigan a giant ___.
18. Kenny's description of the Appalachian Mountains
19. Byron's name for the whirlpool: Wool ____.
21. What Byron had done to his hair

Crossword 3 Answer Key Watsons Go To Birmingham--1963

	1 S	2 Q	U	3 I	R	R	4 E	L	S					
	W		L		O		J		5 Y					
	E		T		6 B		7 M	B	E	A	R	8 D	9 W	
	D		R		E		I		I		K	10 O	V	E	N
	I		A		11 R	E	C	O	R	D		V		L	12 S
	S			T		H		M		13 L	E	14 F	O	U	R
	H					I		I		A		A		M	
			15 K	16 I	N	G		17 N	A	Z	I	18 S		R	M
				C		A		G		Y		C		E	E
		19 P	I	N	E		N		H			A			R
		O		B			20 C	A	R	P		R		21 C	
22 G	O	D		O			M			23 B	Y	R	O	N	
	H			X										N	
						24 N	O	T	E	B	O	O	K		

Across
1. Rufus and Cody thought the ones in Flint were skinny.
7. Dad said they were tickling God's ___ as they drove.
10. Kenny said Birmingham was like one.
11. Dad put a ___ player in the car.
14. Number of girls killed in the church bombing
15. Kenny said Larry was ___ of School.
17. Rufus did not mind being these when playing dinosaurs.
19. Pinnacle of Western Civilization: ___ tree
20. Game Byron and Buphead played with Larry: Great ___ Escape
22. Kenny said Byron was ___ of School.
23. Older brother who helped Kenny at the end of the story
24. Where Momma kept the details of the trip

Down
1. Byron killed bird with ____ Creme
2. Record player was a True-Tone AB-700 ___ Glide
3. Grandma's dear friend: Mr. ___
4. He stole Kenny's dinosaurs: __ Jones
5. Kenny's song: Yakety ___
6. State where Watson family lived.
7. City where Momma originally came from.
8. Byron killed and buried it.
9. Byron thought this was the reason for signing for food.
12. Shortest length of time Byron would be in Alabama
13. Kenny was teased because he had a ___ eye.
16. Momma called Michigan a giant ___.
18. Kenny's description of the Appalachian Mountains
19. Byron's name for the whirlpool: Wool ____.
21. What Byron had done to his hair

Crossword 4 Watsons Go To Birmingham--1963

Across
1. Grandma's dear friend: Mr. ___
5. Dad whistled this tune: Straighten Up and ___ Right
6. Byron thought this was the reason for signing for food.
8. Number of girls killed in the church bombing
10. What Byron had done to his hair
13. Byron killed and buried it.
14. Instead the meeting was like King Kong and ___.
17. Kenny's description of the Appalachian Mountains
20. Rufus did not mind being these when playing dinosaurs.
21. What Kenny brought out of the church
22. Kenny said Byron was ___ of School.
23. Byron's name for the whirlpool: Wool ____.
24. Older brother who helped Kenny at the end of the story
25. Rufus and Cody thought the ones in Flint were skinny.

Down
1. Kenny's friend picked on by other kids
2. Byron said the Wool Pooh was Winnie the Pooh's evil ___.
3. Kenny's song: Yakety ___
4. Dad put a ___ player in the car.
5. Momma said she would burn Byron's.
7. He stole Kenny's dinosaurs: __ Jones
9. Record player was a True-Tone AB-700 ___ Glide
11. Kenny said Birmingham was like one.
12. City where Momma originally came from.
13. Kenny's favorite toys
14. Dad said they were tickling God's ___ as they drove.
15. State where Watson family lived.
16. Pinnacle of Western Civilization: ___ tree
18. Kenny hid behind it every day.
19. Kenny said Larry was ____ of School.

Crossword 4 Answer Key Watsons Go To Birmingham--1963

	1 R	O	B	E	R	2 T			3 Y		4 R		5 F	L	Y	
	U					6 W	E	7 L	F	A	R	E	I			
	8 F	9 O	U	R		I		J		K	10 C	O	N	K		
	U		L			N					O		G			
	S		T				11 O				R		E		12 B	
			R		13 D	O	V	E			D		R		I	
		14 B	15 A	M	B	I		E		16 P		17 S	18 C	A	R	Y
19 K		E		I	N		20 N	A	Z	I	S		O		M	
I		A		C			O			S			U		I	
N		R		H		21 S	H	O	E		E		C		N	
22 G	O	D		I		A					23 P	O	O	H	G	
				G		U									H	
				A		R									A	
24 B	Y	R	O	N		25 S	Q	U	I	R	R	E	L	S	M	

Across
1. Grandma's dear friend: Mr. ___
5. Dad whistled this tune: Straighten Up and ___ Right
6. Byron thought this was the reason for signing for food.
8. Number of girls killed in the church bombing
10. What Byron had done to his hair
13. Byron killed and buried it.
14. Instead the meeting was like King Kong and ___.
17. Kenny's description of the Appalachian Mountains
20. Rufus did not mind being these when playing dinosaurs.
21. What Kenny brought out of the church
22. Kenny said Byron was ___ of School.
23. Byron's name for the whirlpool: Wool ____.
24. Older brother who helped Kenny at the end of the story
25. Rufus and Cody thought the ones in Flint were skinny.

Down
1. Kenny's friend picked on by other kids
2. Byron said the Wool Pooh was Winnie the Pooh's evil ___.
3. Kenny's song: Yakety ___
4. Dad put a ___ player in the car.
5. Momma said she would burn Byron's.
7. He stole Kenny's dinosaurs: ___ Jones
9. Record player was a True-Tone AB-700 ___ Glide
11. Kenny said Birmingham was like one.
12. City where Momma originally came from.
13. Kenny's favorite toys
14. Dad said they were tickling God's ___ as they drove.
15. State where Watson family lived.
16. Pinnacle of Western Civilization: ___ tree
18. Kenny hid behind it every day.
19. Kenny said Larry was ____ of School.

Watsons Go To Birmingham--1963

FINGERS	HOSPITAL	JUVENILE	SHOE	APPALACHIAN
TALKING	WINDOWS	KING	CODY	NOTEBOOK
COUCH	DINOSAURS	FREE SPACE	TOOTHBRSH	SQUIRRELS
BIRMINGHAM	BAMBI	LJ	SWEDISH	SCARY
CARP	RUFUS	BROWN	OVEN	ROBERT

Watsons Go To Birmingham--1963

DROWNED	ULTRA	KENNY	BUPHEAD	BOARDWALK
WEIRD	PINE	BATHROOM	GOD	BEARD
SAVIOR	ALABAMA	FREE SPACE	FLY	WHIRLPOOL
LAYERS	WELFARE	COLLIER	TEETH	LIPLESS
FOUR	PLYMOUTH	DOVE	POOH	RECORD

Watsons Go To Birmingham--1963

FOUR	POOH	GOD	BALD	MITCHELL
SQUIRRELS	BOMB	CHURCH	FLY	SCARY
TOOTHBRSH	BEARD	FREE SPACE	SHOE	ROBERT
BAMBI	GODZILLA	CARP	LJ	WINDOWS
FLINT	KENNY	SAVIOR	BROWN	MICHIGAN

Watsons Go To Birmingham--1963

BOARDWALK	MAGIC	RECORD	LAZY	BIRMINGHAM
KING	SUMMER	OVEN	RUFUS	TALKING
MIRROR	BYRON	FREE SPACE	ALABAMA	ULTRA
LIPLESS	NOTEBOOK	SANDS	JUVENILE	DROWNED
DINOSAURS	MATCHES	BUPHEAD	COLLIER	APPALACHIAN

Watsons Go To Birmingham--1963

MAGIC	DOVE	BEARD	LIPLESS	SHOE
PINE	DROWNED	TOOTHBRSH	WELFARE	CHURCH
MIRROR	SCARY	FREE SPACE	CARP	CODY
ALABAMA	WHIRLPOOL	HOSPITAL	BROWN	KING
FINGERS	LJ	RUFUS	SAVIOR	COLLIER

Watsons Go To Birmingham--1963

BOMB	BIRMINGHAM	RECORD	BOARDWALK	LAZY
SANDS	APPALACHIAN	ICEBOX	TWIN	DINOSAURS
LARRY	FLY	FREE SPACE	JOEY	BAMBI
WINDOWS	GOD	COUCH	BALD	FLINT
PLYMOUTH	TALKING	WEIRD	NAZIS	BATHROOM

Watsons Go To Birmingham--1963

PINE	ULTRA	SQUIRRELS	BYRON	WINDOWS
MIRROR	BIRMINGHAM	BEARD	CHURCH	KENNY
MATCHES	BAMBI	FREE SPACE	ROBERT	APPALACHIAN
LAYERS	TOOTHBRSH	LAZY	COLLIER	RECORD
CARP	GODZILLA	POOH	MITCHELL	BROWN

Watsons Go To Birmingham--1963

ALABAMA	CONK	RUFUS	SUMMER	SWEDISH
TALKING	KING	JUVENILE	YAK	BOMB
BOARDWALK	OVEN	FREE SPACE	TWIN	CODY
NOTEBOOK	DOVE	WHIRLPOOL	LJ	DROWNED
PLYMOUTH	LIPLESS	WEIRD	FINGERS	NAZIS

Watsons Go To Birmingham--1963

MITCHELL	WEIRD	WHIRLPOOL	JOEY	BYRON
BALD	OVEN	SWEDISH	GODZILLA	BAMBI
BEARD	LAZY	FREE SPACE	BIRMINGHAM	FOUR
FINGERS	PLYMOUTH	CONK	ULTRA	YAK
SUMMER	SHOE	TALKING	APPALACHIAN	SCARY

Watsons Go To Birmingham--1963

FLINT	SAVIOR	HOSPITAL	CODY	RUFUS
MIRROR	CHURCH	WINDOWS	TEETH	DOVE
SQUIRRELS	LJ	FREE SPACE	MICHIGAN	SANDS
NAZIS	TWIN	COUCH	COLLIER	MATCHES
LAYERS	ICEBOX	NOTEBOOK	BROWN	BOMB

Watsons Go To Birmingham--1963

LJ	ULTRA	GODZILLA	MIRROR	NOTEBOOK
BOARDWALK	RUFUS	TWIN	CONK	FINGERS
LAYERS	JUVENILE	FREE SPACE	JOEY	POOH
GOD	SAVIOR	TALKING	LARRY	ALABAMA
DROWNED	PLYMOUTH	MICHIGAN	SANDS	FLY

Watsons Go To Birmingham--1963

SQUIRRELS	CHURCH	KENNY	BEARD	PINE
OVEN	KING	SCARY	TOOTHBRSH	BOMB
BATHROOM	APPALACHIAN	FREE SPACE	LIPLESS	BAMBI
FLINT	WEIRD	COUCH	ICEBOX	MITCHELL
CARP	FOUR	LAZY	BALD	RECORD

Watsons Go To Birmingham--1963

SHOE	POOH	SWEDISH	BATHROOM	FOUR
BALD	BAMBI	GOD	ALABAMA	HOSPITAL
OVEN	NAZIS	FREE SPACE	BIRMINGHAM	TEETH
JUVENILE	BOMB	CARP	SQUIRRELS	TWIN
CODY	WELFARE	ROBERT	RUFUS	NOTEBOOK

CARD NO: 69   MARY COLLINS

Watsons Go To Birmingham--1963

BYRON	CHURCH	COLLIER	BROWN	PLYMOUTH
MATCHES	APPALACHIAN	MITCHELL	LAYERS	MICHIGAN
TOOTHBRSH	TALKING	FREE SPACE	LAZY	DOVE
FLINT	RECORD	COUCH	JOEY	KENNY
YAK	SCARY	WHIRLPOOL	SANDS	BUPHEAD

Watsons Go To Birmingham--1963

BUPHEAD	MIRROR	SANDS	GOD	ULTRA
LARRY	TOOTHBRSH	BEARD	TWIN	WELFARE
TALKING	ICEBOX	FREE SPACE	BYRON	COLLIER
GODZILLA	SCARY	LAZY	SUMMER	WINDOWS
LJ	CONK	ROBERT	POOH	JUVENILE

Watsons Go To Birmingham--1963

DROWNED	MITCHELL	ALABAMA	COUCH	DOVE
BAMBI	PINE	APPALACHIAN	BIRMINGHAM	KING
JOEY	HOSPITAL	FREE SPACE	PLYMOUTH	YAK
LIPLESS	SAVIOR	LAYERS	BOARDWALK	SHOE
CARP	FOUR	CHURCH	NOTEBOOK	TEETH

Watsons Go To Birmingham--1963

SCARY	PLYMOUTH	ULTRA	BOARDWALK	SWEDISH
MIRROR	GODZILLA	KENNY	ROBERT	FOUR
RECORD	CONK	FREE SPACE	TWIN	SAVIOR
BATHROOM	NAZIS	OVEN	RUFUS	WEIRD
MICHIGAN	BYRON	SQUIRRELS	BOMB	BIRMINGHAM

Watsons Go To Birmingham--1963

CODY	TEETH	COUCH	WHIRLPOOL	PINE
FINGERS	WINDOWS	BALD	ICEBOX	MITCHELL
LAZY	TOOTHBRSH	FREE SPACE	SHOE	LARRY
MAGIC	GOD	FLINT	JOEY	SUMMER
BROWN	LJ	MATCHES	POOH	BEARD

Watsons Go To Birmingham--1963

MIRROR	CODY	DINOSAURS	COUCH	ICEBOX
ULTRA	SHOE	KENNY	SUMMER	FOUR
RUFUS	LARRY	FREE SPACE	COLLIER	BOARDWALK
PINE	BROWN	ROBERT	CHURCH	TOOTHBRSH
WELFARE	BUPHEAD	WHIRLPOOL	HOSPITAL	NAZIS

Watsons Go To Birmingham--1963

BATHROOM	FLINT	WINDOWS	POOH	BALD
LAYERS	JUVENILE	MITCHELL	CONK	BAMBI
MAGIC	LJ	FREE SPACE	BEARD	SCARY
LAZY	YAK	FINGERS	TALKING	PLYMOUTH
TEETH	BYRON	BIRMINGHAM	GODZILLA	FLY

Watsons Go To Birmingham--1963

CONK	TWIN	NAZIS	BIRMINGHAM	LIPLESS
SHOE	LAZY	BALD	SWEDISH	ALABAMA
WHIRLPOOL	RUFUS	FREE SPACE	DROWNED	APPALACHIAN
DINOSAURS	MITCHELL	FLY	NOTEBOOK	GOD
MICHIGAN	LAYERS	ULTRA	BATHROOM	YAK

Watsons Go To Birmingham--1963

PLYMOUTH	CODY	SUMMER	KING	SAVIOR
KENNY	SQUIRRELS	OVEN	CHURCH	LJ
WEIRD	WELFARE	FREE SPACE	SANDS	PINE
BYRON	ROBERT	FOUR	BOMB	WINDOWS
SCARY	BEARD	MIRROR	HOSPITAL	COLLIER

Watsons Go To Birmingham--1963

BOARDWALK	BEARD	WEIRD	PINE	RECORD
TOOTHBRSH	NAZIS	APPALACHIAN	CARP	BIRMINGHAM
GODZILLA	CODY	FREE SPACE	FOUR	SHOE
LIPLESS	OVEN	SQUIRRELS	MAGIC	DOVE
COLLIER	ICEBOX	LAZY	POOH	FLINT

Watsons Go To Birmingham--1963

SCARY	BYRON	COUCH	ROBERT	CHURCH
MICHIGAN	TWIN	KING	DROWNED	NOTEBOOK
SUMMER	BROWN	FREE SPACE	FLY	SAVIOR
CONK	BALD	FINGERS	MIRROR	ULTRA
BUPHEAD	BOMB	JOEY	DINOSAURS	MITCHELL

Watsons Go To Birmingham--1963

BAMBI	COUCH	RECORD	NAZIS	LAZY
JOEY	SWEDISH	LAYERS	PLYMOUTH	COLLIER
BEARD	GOD	FREE SPACE	DOVE	WHIRLPOOL
SAVIOR	SUMMER	BATHROOM	FLINT	BALD
MATCHES	ULTRA	HOSPITAL	SHOE	PINE

Watsons Go To Birmingham--1963

ALABAMA	WEIRD	NOTEBOOK	WELFARE	DROWNED
DINOSAURS	RUFUS	BROWN	TWIN	CHURCH
TALKING	FINGERS	FREE SPACE	SANDS	POOH
BOMB	TOOTHBRSH	CONK	FOUR	LJ
BIRMINGHAM	MAGIC	OVEN	YAK	SQUIRRELS

Watsons Go To Birmingham--1963

HOSPITAL	PLYMOUTH	COLLIER	NOTEBOOK	JOEY
LAYERS	DINOSAURS	FINGERS	KING	OVEN
RUFUS	YAK	FREE SPACE	SUMMER	LJ
NAZIS	MIRROR	SAVIOR	BYRON	ROBERT
GODZILLA	ICEBOX	BIRMINGHAM	TOOTHBRSH	TWIN

Watsons Go To Birmingham--1963

SHOE	MAGIC	COUCH	CONK	BUPHEAD
MATCHES	LIPLESS	RECORD	LARRY	WINDOWS
GOD	SANDS	FREE SPACE	ALABAMA	ULTRA
PINE	SQUIRRELS	SWEDISH	DOVE	BOMB
FLY	MITCHELL	JUVENILE	BEARD	CODY

Watsons Go To Birmingham--1963

PINE	WEIRD	TOOTHBRSH	HOSPITAL	POOH
DINOSAURS	FOUR	GODZILLA	MATCHES	JUVENILE
CHURCH	ROBERT	FREE SPACE	DOVE	LAYERS
WELFARE	ALABAMA	BALD	BIRMINGHAM	FINGERS
SQUIRRELS	COLLIER	CODY	SWEDISH	FLINT

Watsons Go To Birmingham--1963

MICHIGAN	TALKING	LARRY	JOEY	ICEBOX
PLYMOUTH	NOTEBOOK	FLY	COUCH	MIRROR
TWIN	BROWN	FREE SPACE	SHOE	MITCHELL
SANDS	KENNY	ULTRA	RUFUS	DROWNED
BEARD	LJ	SAVIOR	RECORD	APPALACHIAN

Watsons Go To Birmingham--1963

BATHROOM	DOVE	WINDOWS	CHURCH	DROWNED
BEARD	LAZY	TOOTHBRSH	COUCH	NOTEBOOK
CARP	DINOSAURS	FREE SPACE	BIRMINGHAM	NAZIS
SHOE	APPALACHIAN	HOSPITAL	LIPLESS	BOARDWALK
MATCHES	COLLIER	PINE	ALABAMA	JOEY

Watsons Go To Birmingham--1963

FOUR	SCARY	BOMB	BROWN	FLY
MICHIGAN	KENNY	SUMMER	ROBERT	CONK
LARRY	SQUIRRELS	FREE SPACE	BAMBI	JUVENILE
TWIN	BALD	PLYMOUTH	MAGIC	POOH
WEIRD	BUPHEAD	GOD	MIRROR	ICEBOX

Watsons Go To Birmingham Vocabulary

No.	Word	Clue/Definition
1.	AUTOMATICALLY	Done without thought
2.	BOUND	Obligated or certain to do something
3.	CARP	Breed of large fish, including goldfish
4.	CONK	A style that straightens curly hair
5.	CONSCIENCE	Sense of right and wrong
6.	CROUCHED	In a posture low to the ground
7.	CURVEBALLS	Distractions
8.	DAZZLE	Amaze
9.	DETERMINED	Firm; strong-minded
10.	DISPOSITION	Related to mood or temperament
11.	DROWSY	Sleepy; tired
12.	DULL	Not interesting; not exciting
13.	EAVESDROPPING	Listening in when the speaker does not know it
14.	ELECTROCUTED	Died by electric shock
15.	EMULATE	Try to be like someone else
16.	EXECUTED	Put to death
17.	FROSTBITE	Damage to limbs caused by freezing
18.	GENERATE	Produce or make
19.	GNASHING	Clenching; grinding
20.	HAPHAZARDLY	Randomly; not planned
21.	HILARIOUS	Very funny
22.	HOSTILE	Full of hatred or anger
23.	HYPNOTIZED	Put into a trance or sleep-like condition
24.	INCAPABLE	Not able to do something
25.	INFECT	Give a disease to
26.	INTIMIDATE	Create a feeling of fear in someone
27.	JABBERING	Talking very quickly
28.	JIVE	Jazz or swing music
29.	MATURE	Grown-up; adult
30.	MUGS	Faces
31.	MUMBLING	Speaking unclearly in a low voice
32.	NIBBLE	Take small, quick, playful bites
33.	NUMB	Not able to feel emotions
34.	PACE	Speed
35.	PATHETIC	Sad; causing feelings of pity
36.	PEON	Very low-paid worker
37.	PUNCTUAL	On time
38.	RABIES	Disease of warm-blooded animals
39.	SANITATION	Related to health and cleanliness
40.	SCOWL	Angry expression
41.	SENIORITY	Having greater age or higher rank
42.	SLEW	A large number
43.	SNITCH	Someone who tells on others
44.	SOBBY	Full of tears; crying
45.	SQUARE	Out of touch; old fashioned
46.	STAGGERED	Walked unsteadily
47.	STILL	Having no motion
48.	STINGY	Not generous; not willing to share
49.	STUNT	Stop; restrict
50.	SURVIVED	Stayed alive
51.	THUGS	Gangsters; violent criminals

Watsons Go To Birmingham Vocabulary

No.	Word	Clue/Definition
52.	TOLERATE	Put up with
53.	TORTURE	To give pain or make another suffer
54.	TRAITOR	One who does something disloyal
55.	TRESPASSING	Going to a place without permission
56.	ULTIMATE	Highest quality
57.	VITAL	Very important
58.	WAILING	Crying
59.	WELFARE	Aid in the form of money and other benefits
60.	WHIRLPOOL	A spiraling current of water
61.	WILIER	More clever or deceiving

Vocabulary Fill In The Blanks 1 Watsons Go To Birmingham--1963

_____ 1. A spiraling current of water
_____ 2. Done without thought
_____ 3. To give pain or make another suffer
_____ 4. Create a feeling of fear in someone
_____ 5. Put into a trance or sleep-like condition
_____ 6. Produce or make
_____ 7. Angry expression
_____ 8. A style that straightens curly hair
_____ 9. Clenching; grinding
_____ 10. Related to health and cleanliness
_____ 11. Speed
_____ 12. Sense of right and wrong
_____ 13. More clever or deceiving
_____ 14. Randomly; not planned
_____ 15. On time
_____ 16. Try to be like someone else
_____ 17. Out of touch; old fashioned
_____ 18. Very important
_____ 19. Sad; causing feelings of pity
_____ 20. Stop; restrict
_____ 21. Full of tears; crying
_____ 22. A large number
_____ 23. Not able to do something
_____ 24. Going to a place without permission

Vocabulary Fill In The Blanks 1 Answer Key Watsons Go To Birmingham--1963

WHIRLPOOL	1. A spiraling current of water
AUTOMATICALLY	2. Done without thought
TORTURE	3. To give pain or make another suffer
INTIMIDATE	4. Create a feeling of fear in someone
HYPNOTIZED	5. Put into a trance or sleep-like condition
GENERATE	6. Produce or make
SCOWL	7. Angry expression
CONK	8. A style that straightens curly hair
GNASHING	9. Clenching; grinding
SANITATION	10. Related to health and cleanliness
PACE	11. Speed
CONSCIENCE	12. Sense of right and wrong
WILIER	13. More clever or deceiving
HAPHAZARDLY	14. Randomly; not planned
PUNCTUAL	15. On time
EMULATE	16. Try to be like someone else
SQUARE	17. Out of touch; old fashioned
VITAL	18. Very important
PATHETIC	19. Sad; causing feelings of pity
STUNT	20. Stop; restrict
SOBBY	21. Full of tears; crying
SLEW	22. A large number
INCAPABLE	23. Not able to do something
TRESPASSING	24. Going to a place without permission

Vocabulary Fill In The Blanks 2 Watsons Go To Birmingham--1963

_____ 1. Related to health and cleanliness

_____ 2. Full of tears; crying

_____ 3. Not able to do something

_____ 4. Obligated or certain to do something

_____ 5. Listening in when the speaker does not know it

_____ 6. Firm; strong-minded

_____ 7. Distractions

_____ 8. A large number

_____ 9. Not interesting; not exciting

_____ 10. Sense of right and wrong

_____ 11. Talking very quickly

_____ 12. Walked unsteadily

_____ 13. Create a feeling of fear in someone

_____ 14. Stop; restrict

_____ 15. One who does something disloyal

_____ 16. Grown-up; adult

_____ 17. To give pain or make another suffer

_____ 18. Out of touch; old fashioned

_____ 19. Someone who tells on others

_____ 20. Having no motion

_____ 21. Very low-paid worker

_____ 22. Having greater age or higher rank

_____ 23. Try to be like someone else

_____ 24. Related to mood or temperament

Vocabulary Fill In The Blanks 2 Answer Key Watsons Go To Birmingham--1963

SANITATION	1. Related to health and cleanliness
SOBBY	2. Full of tears; crying
INCAPABLE	3. Not able to do something
BOUND	4. Obligated or certain to do something
EAVESDROPPING	5. Listening in when the speaker does not know it
DETERMINED	6. Firm; strong-minded
CURVEBALLS	7. Distractions
SLEW	8. A large number
DULL	9. Not interesting; not exciting
CONSCIENCE	10. Sense of right and wrong
JABBERING	11. Talking very quickly
STAGGERED	12. Walked unsteadily
INTIMIDATE	13. Create a feeling of fear in someone
STUNT	14. Stop; restrict
TRAITOR	15. One who does something disloyal
MATURE	16. Grown-up; adult
TORTURE	17. To give pain or make another suffer
SQUARE	18. Out of touch; old fashioned
SNITCH	19. Someone who tells on others
STILL	20. Having no motion
PEON	21. Very low-paid worker
SENIORITY	22. Having greater age or higher rank
EMULATE	23. Try to be like someone else
DISPOSITION	24. Related to mood or temperament

Vocabulary Fill In The Blanks 3 Watsons Go To Birmingham--1963

_____ 1. Grown-up; adult

_____ 2. Related to mood or temperament

_____ 3. Aid in the form of money and other benefits

_____ 4. Highest quality

_____ 5. Listening in when the speaker does not know it

_____ 6. On time

_____ 7. One who does something disloyal

_____ 8. Done without thought

_____ 9. Faces

_____ 10. Obligated or certain to do something

_____ 11. Damage to limbs caused by freezing

_____ 12. Talking very quickly

_____ 13. Sense of right and wrong

_____ 14. Someone who tells on others

_____ 15. Very low-paid worker

_____ 16. Create a feeling of fear in someone

_____ 17. To give pain or make another suffer

_____ 18. Full of hatred or anger

_____ 19. Amaze

_____ 20. Related to health and cleanliness

_____ 21. Clenching; grinding

_____ 22. Stayed alive

_____ 23. Speed

_____ 24. Give a disease to

Vocabulary Fill In The Blanks 3 Answer Key Watsons Go To Birmingham--1963

MATURE	1. Grown-up; adult
DISPOSITION	2. Related to mood or temperament
WELFARE	3. Aid in the form of money and other benefits
ULTIMATE	4. Highest quality
EAVESDROPPING	5. Listening in when the speaker does not know it
PUNCTUAL	6. On time
TRAITOR	7. One who does something disloyal
AUTOMATICALLY	8. Done without thought
MUGS	9. Faces
BOUND	10. Obligated or certain to do something
FROSTBITE	11. Damage to limbs caused by freezing
JABBERING	12. Talking very quickly
CONSCIENCE	13. Sense of right and wrong
SNITCH	14. Someone who tells on others
PEON	15. Very low-paid worker
INTIMIDATE	16. Create a feeling of fear in someone
TORTURE	17. To give pain or make another suffer
HOSTILE	18. Full of hatred or anger
DAZZLE	19. Amaze
SANITATION	20. Related to health and cleanliness
GNASHING	21. Clenching; grinding
SURVIVED	22. Stayed alive
PACE	23. Speed
INFECT	24. Give a disease to

Vocabulary Fill In The Blanks 4 Watsons Go To Birmingham--1963

_____ 1. Amaze

_____ 2. Related to health and cleanliness

_____ 3. Distractions

_____ 4. Died by electric shock

_____ 5. Not able to feel emotions

_____ 6. Clenching; grinding

_____ 7. Crying

_____ 8. Put up with

_____ 9. On time

_____ 10. Put into a trance or sleep-like condition

_____ 11. Highest quality

_____ 12. Done without thought

_____ 13. Very important

_____ 14. Related to mood or temperament

_____ 15. Create a feeling of fear in someone

_____ 16. Try to be like someone else

_____ 17. Having no motion

_____ 18. Faces

_____ 19. Not generous; not willing to share

_____ 20. Someone who tells on others

_____ 21. Stayed alive

_____ 22. Sense of right and wrong

_____ 23. Aid in the form of money and other benefits

_____ 24. Listening in when the speaker does not know it

Vocabulary Fill In The Blanks 4 Answer Key Watsons Go To Birmingham--1963

DAZZLE	1. Amaze
SANITATION	2. Related to health and cleanliness
CURVEBALLS	3. Distractions
ELECTROCUTED	4. Died by electric shock
NUMB	5. Not able to feel emotions
GNASHING	6. Clenching; grinding
WAILING	7. Crying
TOLERATE	8. Put up with
PUNCTUAL	9. On time
HYPNOTIZED	10. Put into a trance or sleep-like condition
ULTIMATE	11. Highest quality
AUTOMATICALLY	12. Done without thought
VITAL	13. Very important
DISPOSITION	14. Related to mood or temperament
INTIMIDATE	15. Create a feeling of fear in someone
EMULATE	16. Try to be like someone else
STILL	17. Having no motion
MUGS	18. Faces
STINGY	19. Not generous; not willing to share
SNITCH	20. Someone who tells on others
SURVIVED	21. Stayed alive
CONSCIENCE	22. Sense of right and wrong
WELFARE	23. Aid in the form of money and other benefits
EAVESDROPPING	24. Listening in when the speaker does not know it

Copyrighted

Vocabulary Matching 1 Watsons Go To Birmingham--1963

___ 1. TRAITOR   A. Give a disease to
___ 2. CONSCIENCE   B. Someone who tells on others
___ 3. DAZZLE   C. Done without thought
___ 4. SNITCH   D. Angry expression
___ 5. HOSTILE   E. Stop; restrict
___ 6. PEON   F. Listening in when the speaker does not know it
___ 7. JABBERING   G. One who does something disloyal
___ 8. DETERMINED   H. Crying
___ 9. TORTURE   I. Stayed alive
___10. STINGY   J. Very low-paid worker
___11. HAPHAZARDLY   K. Put to death
___12. STILL   L. Out of touch; old fashioned
___13. INFECT   M. Produce or make
___14. SCOWL   N. Firm; strong-minded
___15. EXECUTED   O. Grown-up; adult
___16. WAILING   P. To give pain or make another suffer
___17. SQUARE   Q. Talking very quickly
___18. GENERATE   R. Full of hatred or anger
___19. MATURE   S. More clever or deceiving
___20. AUTOMATICALLY   T. Sense of right and wrong
___21. SOBBY   U. Full of tears; crying
___22. WILIER   V. Not generous; not willing to share
___23. EAVESDROPPING   W. Randomly; not planned
___24. STUNT   X. Amaze
___25. SURVIVED   Y. Having no motion

Vocabulary Matching 1 Answer Key Watsons Go To Birmingham--1963

G - 1. TRAITOR	A.	Give a disease to
T - 2. CONSCIENCE	B.	Someone who tells on others
X - 3. DAZZLE	C.	Done without thought
B - 4. SNITCH	D.	Angry expression
R - 5. HOSTILE	E.	Stop; restrict
J - 6. PEON	F.	Listening in when the speaker does not know it
Q - 7. JABBERING	G.	One who does something disloyal
N - 8. DETERMINED	H.	Crying
P - 9. TORTURE	I.	Stayed alive
V - 10. STINGY	J.	Very low-paid worker
W - 11. HAPHAZARDLY	K.	Put to death
Y - 12. STILL	L.	Out of touch; old fashioned
A - 13. INFECT	M.	Produce or make
D - 14. SCOWL	N.	Firm; strong-minded
K - 15. EXECUTED	O.	Grown-up; adult
H - 16. WAILING	P.	To give pain or make another suffer
L - 17. SQUARE	Q.	Talking very quickly
M - 18. GENERATE	R.	Full of hatred or anger
O - 19. MATURE	S.	More clever or deceiving
C - 20. AUTOMATICALLY	T.	Sense of right and wrong
U - 21. SOBBY	U.	Full of tears; crying
S - 22. WILIER	V.	Not generous; not willing to share
F - 23. EAVESDROPPING	W.	Randomly; not planned
E - 24. STUNT	X.	Amaze
I - 25. SURVIVED	Y.	Having no motion

Vocabulary Matching 2 Watsons Go To Birmingham--1963

___ 1. PATHETIC   A. A spiraling current of water

___ 2. NIBBLE   B. Full of tears; crying

___ 3. WHIRLPOOL   C. Put into a trance or sleep-like condition

___ 4. DAZZLE   D. Sad; causing feelings of pity

___ 5. SENIORITY   E. Aid in the form of money and other benefits

___ 6. SOBBY   F. Faces

___ 7. CROUCHED   G. Put up with

___ 8. SCOWL   H. Speed

___ 9. PEON   I. Amaze

___10. HOSTILE   J. Full of hatred or anger

___11. WELFARE   K. Not able to do something

___12. STILL   L. Someone who tells on others

___13. TOLERATE   M. In a posture low to the ground

___14. ULTIMATE   N. To give pain or make another suffer

___15. MUGS   O. Breed of large fish, including goldfish

___16. INCAPABLE   P. Distractions

___17. CURVEBALLS   Q. Crying

___18. JABBERING   R. Having greater age or higher rank

___19. WAILING   S. Take small, quick, playful bites

___20. TORTURE   T. Angry expression

___21. JIVE   U. Talking very quickly

___22. SNITCH   V. Highest quality

___23. HYPNOTIZED   W. Very low-paid worker

___24. CARP   X. Jazz or swing music

___25. PACE   Y. Having no motion

Vocabulary Matching 2 Answer Key Watsons Go To Birmingham--1963

D - 1. PATHETIC		A. A spiraling current of water
S - 2. NIBBLE		B. Full of tears; crying
A - 3. WHIRLPOOL		C. Put into a trance or sleep-like condition
I - 4. DAZZLE		D. Sad; causing feelings of pity
R - 5. SENIORITY		E. Aid in the form of money and other benefits
B - 6. SOBBY		F. Faces
M - 7. CROUCHED		G. Put up with
T - 8. SCOWL		H. Speed
W - 9. PEON		I. Amaze
J - 10. HOSTILE		J. Full of hatred or anger
E - 11. WELFARE		K. Not able to do something
Y - 12. STILL		L. Someone who tells on others
G - 13. TOLERATE		M. In a posture low to the ground
V - 14. ULTIMATE		N. To give pain or make another suffer
F - 15. MUGS		O. Breed of large fish, including goldfish
K - 16. INCAPABLE		P. Distractions
P - 17. CURVEBALLS		Q. Crying
U - 18. JABBERING		R. Having greater age or higher rank
Q - 19. WAILING		S. Take small, quick, playful bites
N - 20. TORTURE		T. Angry expression
X - 21. JIVE		U. Talking very quickly
L - 22. SNITCH		V. Highest quality
C - 23. HYPNOTIZED		W. Very low-paid worker
O - 24. CARP		X. Jazz or swing music
H - 25. PACE		Y. Having no motion

Vocabulary Matching 3 Watsons Go To Birmingham--1963

___ 1. INFECT   A. Full of tears; crying
___ 2. JIVE   B. Breed of large fish, including goldfish
___ 3. NIBBLE   C. Sad; causing feelings of pity
___ 4. MATURE   D. Take small, quick, playful bites
___ 5. STILL   E. Gangsters; violent criminals
___ 6. INTIMIDATE   F. In a posture low to the ground
___ 7. SQUARE   G. Amaze
___ 8. CROUCHED   H. Sleepy; tired
___ 9. SOBBY   I. Grown-up; adult
___10. GNASHING   J. Distractions
___11. RABIES   K. Out of touch; old fashioned
___12. SANITATION   L. Give a disease to
___13. PEON   M. To give pain or make another suffer
___14. MUGS   N. Disease of warm-blooded animals
___15. CARP   O. One who does something disloyal
___16. TORTURE   P. Create a feeling of fear in someone
___17. DROWSY   Q. Clenching; grinding
___18. THUGS   R. Very low-paid worker
___19. TOLERATE   S. Having no motion
___20. BOUND   T. Not generous; not willing to share
___21. CURVEBALLS   U. Obligated or certain to do something
___22. TRAITOR   V. Jazz or swing music
___23. STINGY   W. Put up with
___24. DAZZLE   X. Related to health and cleanliness
___25. PATHETIC   Y. Faces

Vocabulary Matching 3 Answer Key Watsons Go To Birmingham--1963

L - 1. INFECT	A.	Full of tears; crying
V - 2. JIVE	B.	Breed of large fish, including goldfish
D - 3. NIBBLE	C.	Sad; causing feelings of pity
I - 4. MATURE	D.	Take small, quick, playful bites
S - 5. STILL	E.	Gangsters; violent criminals
P - 6. INTIMIDATE	F.	In a posture low to the ground
K - 7. SQUARE	G.	Amaze
F - 8. CROUCHED	H.	Sleepy; tired
A - 9. SOBBY	I.	Grown-up; adult
Q - 10. GNASHING	J.	Distractions
N - 11. RABIES	K.	Out of touch; old fashioned
X - 12. SANITATION	L.	Give a disease to
R - 13. PEON	M.	To give pain or make another suffer
Y - 14. MUGS	N.	Disease of warm-blooded animals
B - 15. CARP	O.	One who does something disloyal
M - 16. TORTURE	P.	Create a feeling of fear in someone
H - 17. DROWSY	Q.	Clenching; grinding
E - 18. THUGS	R.	Very low-paid worker
W - 19. TOLERATE	S.	Having no motion
U - 20. BOUND	T.	Not generous; not willing to share
J - 21. CURVEBALLS	U.	Obligated or certain to do something
O - 22. TRAITOR	V.	Jazz or swing music
T - 23. STINGY	W.	Put up with
G - 24. DAZZLE	X.	Related to health and cleanliness
C - 25. PATHETIC	Y.	Faces

Vocabulary Matching 4 Watsons Go To Birmingham--1963

___ 1. INCAPABLE   A. Not able to do something
___ 2. FROSTBITE   B. Having greater age or higher rank
___ 3. HYPNOTIZED   C. Stop; restrict
___ 4. ULTIMATE   D. Going to a place without permission
___ 5. VITAL   E. Aid in the form of money and other benefits
___ 6. THUGS   F. A large number
___ 7. TRAITOR   G. Highest quality
___ 8. TRESPASSING   H. Randomly; not planned
___ 9. SQUARE   I. Not interesting; not exciting
___10. SENIORITY   J. Put into a trance or sleep-like condition
___11. NUMB   K. Gangsters; violent criminals
___12. SURVIVED   L. Out of touch; old fashioned
___13. DULL   M. Obligated or certain to do something
___14. MUMBLING   N. Related to mood or temperament
___15. TORTURE   O. To give pain or make another suffer
___16. DISPOSITION   P. Stayed alive
___17. STUNT   Q. Not able to feel emotions
___18. MUGS   R. More clever or deceiving
___19. SLEW   S. Very important
___20. HAPHAZARDLY   T. Damage to limbs caused by freezing
___21. BOUND   U. One who does something disloyal
___22. WELFARE   V. Distractions
___23. CURVEBALLS   W. Faces
___24. STAGGERED   X. Speaking unclearly in a low voice
___25. WILIER   Y. Walked unsteadily

Vocabulary Matching 4 Answer Key Watsons Go To Birmingham--1963

A - 1. INCAPABLE		A. Not able to do something
T - 2. FROSTBITE		B. Having greater age or higher rank
J - 3. HYPNOTIZED		C. Stop; restrict
G - 4. ULTIMATE		D. Going to a place without permission
S - 5. VITAL		E. Aid in the form of money and other benefits
K - 6. THUGS		F. A large number
U - 7. TRAITOR		G. Highest quality
D - 8. TRESPASSING		H. Randomly; not planned
L - 9. SQUARE		I. Not interesting; not exciting
B - 10. SENIORITY		J. Put into a trance or sleep-like condition
Q - 11. NUMB		K. Gangsters; violent criminals
P - 12. SURVIVED		L. Out of touch; old fashioned
I - 13. DULL		M. Obligated or certain to do something
X - 14. MUMBLING		N. Related to mood or temperament
O - 15. TORTURE		O. To give pain or make another suffer
N - 16. DISPOSITION		P. Stayed alive
C - 17. STUNT		Q. Not able to feel emotions
W - 18. MUGS		R. More clever or deceiving
F - 19. SLEW		S. Very important
H - 20. HAPHAZARDLY		T. Damage to limbs caused by freezing
M - 21. BOUND		U. One who does something disloyal
E - 22. WELFARE		V. Distractions
V - 23. CURVEBALLS		W. Faces
Y - 24. STAGGERED		X. Speaking unclearly in a low voice
R - 25. WILIER		Y. Walked unsteadily

Vocabulary Magic Squares 1 Watsons Go To Birmingham--1963

Match the definition with the vocabulary word. Put your answers in the magic squares below. When your answers are correct, all columns and rows will add to the same number.

A. WILIER
B. TRESPASSING
C. DROWSY
D. SQUARE
E. INFECT
F. WELFARE
G. FROSTBITE
H. STINGY
I. GENERATE
J. MUGS
K. PEON
L. WHIRLPOOL
M. INCAPABLE
N. CARP
O. INTIMIDATE
P. GNASHING

1. Not able to do something
2. Aid in the form of money and other benefits
3. Not generous; not willing to share
4. Create a feeling of fear in someone
5. A spiraling current of water
6. Sleepy; tired
7. More clever or deceiving
8. Faces
9. Very low-paid worker
10. Out of touch; old fashioned
11. Going to a place without permission
12. Produce or make
13. Breed of large fish, including goldfish
14. Give a disease to
15. Damage to limbs caused by freezing
16. Clenching; grinding

A=	B=	C=	D=
E=	F=	G=	H=
I=	J=	K=	L=
M=	N=	O=	P=

Vocabulary Magic Squares 1 Answer Key Watsons Go To Birmingham--1963

Match the definition with the vocabulary word. Put your answers in the magic squares below. When your answers are correct, all columns and rows will add to the same number.

A. WILIER
B. TRESPASSING
C. DROWSY
D. SQUARE
E. INFECT
F. WELFARE
G. FROSTBITE
H. STINGY
I. GENERATE
J. MUGS
K. PEON
L. WHIRLPOOL
M. INCAPABLE
N. CARP
O. INTIMIDATE
P. GNASHING

1. Not able to do something
2. Aid in the form of money and other benefits
3. Not generous; not willing to share
4. Create a feeling of fear in someone
5. A spiraling current of water
6. Sleepy; tired
7. More clever or deceiving
8. Faces
9. Very low-paid worker
10. Out of touch; old fashioned
11. Going to a place without permission
12. Produce or make
13. Breed of large fish, including goldfish
14. Give a disease to
15. Damage to limbs caused by freezing
16. Clenching; grinding

A=7	B=11	C=6	D=10
E=14	F=2	G=15	H=3
I=12	J=8	K=9	L=5
M=1	N=13	O=4	P=16

Vocabulary Magic Squares 2 Watsons Go To Birmingham--1963

Match the definition with the vocabulary word. Put your answers in the magic squares below. When your answers are correct, all columns and rows will add to the same number.

A. ELECTROCUTED G. VITAL   M. BOUND
B. STILL   H. NUMB   N. DAZZLE
C. SQUARE   I. INFECT   O. DETERMINED
D. CROUCHED   J. FROSTBITE   P. NIBBLE
E. SURVIVED   K. WAILING
F. AUTOMATICALLY L. HILARIOUS

1. Done without thought
2. Give a disease to
3. Firm; strong-minded
4. In a posture low to the ground
5. Obligated or certain to do something
6. Having no motion
7. Not able to feel emotions
8. Crying
9. Out of touch; old fashioned
10. Take small, quick, playful bites
11. Damage to limbs caused by freezing
12. Stayed alive
13. Very funny
14. Very important
15. Died by electric shock
16. Amaze

A=	B=	C=	D=
E=	F=	G=	H=
I=	J=	K=	L=
M=	N=	O=	P=

Vocabulary Magic Squares 2 Answer Key Watsons Go To Birmingham--1963

Match the definition with the vocabulary word. Put your answers in the magic squares below. When your answers are correct, all columns and rows will add to the same number.

A. ELECTROCUTED G. VITAL   M. BOUND
B. STILL   H. NUMB   N. DAZZLE
C. SQUARE   I. INFECT   O. DETERMINED
D. CROUCHED   J. FROSTBITE   P. NIBBLE
E. SURVIVED   K. WAILING
F. AUTOMATICALLY L. HILARIOUS

1. Done without thought
2. Give a disease to
3. Firm; strong-minded
4. In a posture low to the ground
5. Obligated or certain to do something
6. Having no motion
7. Not able to feel emotions
8. Crying
9. Out of touch; old fashioned
10. Take small, quick, playful bites
11. Damage to limbs caused by freezing
12. Stayed alive
13. Very funny
14. Very important
15. Died by electric shock
16. Amaze

A=15	B=6	C=9	D=4
E=12	F=1	G=14	H=7
I=2	J=11	K=8	L=13
M=5	N=16	O=3	P=10

Vocabulary Magic Squares 3 Watsons Go To Birmingham--1963

Match the definition with the vocabulary word. Put your answers in the magic squares below. When your answers are correct, all columns and rows will add to the same number.

A. THUGS
B. EXECUTED
C. STAGGERED
D. RABIES
E. DULL
F. EAVESDROPPING
G. ELECTROCUTED
H. HYPNOTIZED
I. CROUCHED
J. DISPOSITION
K. SQUARE
L. SURVIVED
M. HAPHAZARDLY
N. MUGS
O. SCOWL
P. NUMB

1. Walked unsteadily
2. Related to mood or temperament
3. Listening in when the speaker does not know it
4. Angry expression
5. Not able to feel emotions
6. Not interesting; not exciting
7. In a posture low to the ground
8. Disease of warm-blooded animals
9. Randomly; not planned
10. Put into a trance or sleep-like condition
11. Stayed alive
12. Gangsters; violent criminals
13. Put to death
14. Out of touch; old fashioned
15. Died by electric shock
16. Faces

A=	B=	C=	D=
E=	F=	G=	H=
I=	J=	K=	L=
M=	N=	O=	P=

Vocabulary Magic Squares 3 Answer Key Watsons Go To Birmingham--1963

Match the definition with the vocabulary word. Put your answers in the magic squares below. When your answers are correct, all columns and rows will add to the same number.

A. THUGS
B. EXECUTED
C. STAGGERED
D. RABIES
E. DULL
F. EAVESDROPPING
G. ELECTROCUTED
H. HYPNOTIZED
I. CROUCHED
J. DISPOSITION
K. SQUARE
L. SURVIVED
M. HAPHAZARDLY
N. MUGS
O. SCOWL
P. NUMB

1. Walked unsteadily
2. Related to mood or temperament
3. Listening in when the speaker does not know it
4. Angry expression
5. Not able to feel emotions
6. Not interesting; not exciting
7. In a posture low to the ground
8. Disease of warm-blooded animals
9. Randomly; not planned
10. Put into a trance or sleep-like condition
11. Stayed alive
12. Gangsters; violent criminals
13. Put to death
14. Out of touch; old fashioned
15. Died by electric shock
16. Faces

A=12	B=13	C=1	D=8
E=6	F=3	G=15	H=10
I=7	J=2	K=14	L=11
M=9	N=16	O=4	P=5

Vocabulary Magic Squares 4 Watsons Go To Birmingham--1963

Match the definition with the vocabulary word. Put your answers in the magic squares below. When your answers are correct, all columns and rows will add to the same number.

A. VITAL
B. GENERATE
C. EMULATE
D. WILIER
E. EAVESDROPPING
F. MUGS
G. HOSTILE
H. CONK
I. TRESPASSING
J. STAGGERED
K. SOBBY
L. CURVEBALLS
M. JABBERING
N. HYPNOTIZED
O. INTIMIDATE
P. SANITATION

1. Try to be like someone else
2. Walked unsteadily
3. Faces
4. Create a feeling of fear in someone
5. Related to health and cleanliness
6. Listening in when the speaker does not know it
7. Going to a place without permission
8. More clever or deceiving
9. Talking very quickly
10. A style that straightens curly hair
11. Distractions
12. Very important
13. Produce or make
14. Full of tears; crying
15. Full of hatred or anger
16. Put into a trance or sleep-like condition

A=	B=	C=	D=
E=	F=	G=	H=
I=	J=	K=	L=
M=	N=	O=	P=

Vocabulary Magic Squares 4 Answer Key Watsons Go To Birmingham--1963

Match the definition with the vocabulary word. Put your answers in the magic squares below. When your answers are correct, all columns and rows will add to the same number.

A. VITAL
B. GENERATE
C. EMULATE
D. WILIER
E. EAVESDROPPING
F. MUGS
G. HOSTILE
H. CONK
I. TRESPASSING
J. STAGGERED
K. SOBBY
L. CURVEBALLS
M. JABBERING
N. HYPNOTIZED
O. INTIMIDATE
P. SANITATION

1. Try to be like someone else
2. Walked unsteadily
3. Faces
4. Create a feeling of fear in someone
5. Related to health and cleanliness
6. Listening in when the speaker does not know it
7. Going to a place without permission
8. More clever or deceiving
9. Talking very quickly
10. A style that straightens curly hair
11. Distractions
12. Very important
13. Produce or make
14. Full of tears; crying
15. Full of hatred or anger
16. Put into a trance or sleep-like condition

A=12	B=13	C=1	D=8
E=6	F=3	G=15	H=10
I=7	J=2	K=14	L=11
M=9	N=16	O=4	P=5

Vocabulary Word Search 1 Watsons Go To Birmingham--1963

```
H A P H A Z A R D L Y B B O S X S Z E H
N Y L W J A B B E R I N G Z U X T V X M
P Q P M P D R B V F O V W J O Y I S E V
G C T N S P E S I S Q W Y S I J N D C F
C A R P O D I F V N B Z S G R T G D U D
G T E O Z T L P R I C W P Y A H Y E T B
E O S X U B I M U T S A P M L U J R E W
N R P G F C W Z S C T I P L I G H E D C
E T A J R L H F E H B L Q A H S C G M J
R U S D O I G E E D N I G K B X N G D K
A S S K S L N T D C O N K W E L F A R E
T E I G T I I F V D I G S S X A E T Q V
E B N G B C T Z E L T K L B Z T R S H R
C W G B I W T T B C A D G Q D I P B Z P
V E L K T C Z M M A T U R E G V P U L Q
B M C E C U W L R I L L N D D D L O B
G Q T U J M H Q A O N P I Z A X N T O V
C Y X S L L O N U T A H A Z N S U I P D
M H G L W A S S T I S L Z C O W O M L S
A U T O M A T I C A L L Y S E I B A R K
M P C P J I I E N R E U V L P M R T I L
S S W F L S L G U T X D S Q U A R E H Y
F G W L K P E W P Y H W T N U T S W W G
```

AUTOMATICALLY	HAPHAZARDLY	PACE	STINGY
BOUND	HILARIOUS	PATHETIC	STUNT
CARP	HOSTILE	PEON	SURVIVED
CONK	HYPNOTIZED	PUNCTUAL	THUGS
CROUCHED	INCAPABLE	RABIES	TORTURE
DAZZLE	INFECT	SANITATION	TRAITOR
DROWSY	JABBERING	SCOWL	TRESPASSING
DULL	JIVE	SLEW	ULTIMATE
EMULATE	MATURE	SNITCH	VITAL
EXECUTED	MUGS	SOBBY	WAILING
FROSTBITE	MUMBLING	SQUARE	WELFARE
GENERATE	NIBBLE	STAGGERED	WHIRLPOOL
GNASHING	NUMB	STILL	WILIER

Vocabulary Word Search 1 Answer Key Watsons Go To Birmingham--1963

AUTOMATICALLY	HAPHAZARDLY	PACE	STINGY
BOUND	HILARIOUS	PATHETIC	STUNT
CARP	HOSTILE	PEON	SURVIVED
CONK	HYPNOTIZED	PUNCTUAL	THUGS
CROUCHED	INCAPABLE	RABIES	TORTURE
DAZZLE	INFECT	SANITATION	TRAITOR
DROWSY	JABBERING	SCOWL	TRESPASSING
DULL	JIVE	SLEW	ULTIMATE
EMULATE	MATURE	SNITCH	VITAL
EXECUTED	MUGS	SOBBY	WAILING
FROSTBITE	MUMBLING	SQUARE	WELFARE
GENERATE	NIBBLE	STAGGERED	WHIRLPOOL
GNASHING	NUMB	STILL	WILIER

Vocabulary Word Search 2 Watsons Go To Birmingham--1963

```
P U N C T U A L E R A U Q S F G S D S Y
T O R T U R E X H W Q L T R E A D E J
P R T D E R E G G A T S G O O N N B N X
S F A M C C M S C H M C Y L S E I M I Q
D T Q I U O F B P R G L H E T R T P O T
Y F U T T R N S P A L G O R B A A D R X
C H E N P O G S T A S T S A I T T I I D
W D S P T U R M C S Z S T T T E I S T S
G H O W H S Z I D I C N I E E R O P Y N
N F B T N B T Y E M E B L N S U N O R R
I Z B D L A G H H U R N E X G T X S J H
R E Y N M E W H C M S S C V L A G I C B
E J M O P L L W U B S T H E W M K T Q N
B W T U K Z L P O L T I S M O C I I H N
B U E U L Z W R R I D N U N C N O O D V
A S E L B A P A C N I G N A S H I N G M
J U W T F D T C I G S Y O L R N U I K G
J R I I P A D E T L T X E S F O S B N X
S V L M S Y R N E J I W P E B J T B U K
R I I A S Z O E H D Y N C I P I I L M Q
T V E T Z V W L T S U T G B A V L E B G
K E R E A K S K A Y N L B A C E L H S G
S D X V Q L Y T P G M V L R E T R G Z D
```

AUTOMATICALLY	GENERATE	PATHETIC	STINGY
BOUND	GNASHING	PEON	STUNT
CARP	HOSTILE	PUNCTUAL	SURVIVED
CONK	INCAPABLE	RABIES	THUGS
CONSCIENCE	INFECT	SANITATION	TOLERATE
CROUCHED	JABBERING	SCOWL	TORTURE
DAZZLE	JIVE	SENIORITY	TRAITOR
DISPOSITION	MATURE	SLEW	TRESPASSING
DROWSY	MUGS	SNITCH	ULTIMATE
DULL	MUMBLING	SOBBY	VITAL
EMULATE	NIBBLE	SQUARE	WAILING
EXECUTED	NUMB	STAGGERED	WELFARE
FROSTBITE	PACE	STILL	WILIER

Vocabulary Word Search 2 Answer Key Watsons Go To Birmingham--1963

```
P U N C T U A L E R A U Q S   F   G   S       S
T O R T U R E X             T   R   E       S E
  R   D E R E G G A T S     O   O   N       N
S A     C C     S       Y   L   S   E       I
  T     I U   P         L   H   T   R       I O
    U   T T   N S       A   O   B   A   D   R
    E   E N   O G   S   S   S   I   T   I   I
  D S     T   T U R     C   T   T   E   S   T
G O       H     I   D   I   I   E   R   P   Y
N   B     T         E M     L   N   T   O
I   B       A       H C     N E G   A   S   H
R E   Y   M E       C M     S   L   M   I   C
E   M O     L       U B     C E W   C   T   
B W T U     Z   P   O L     O M O   N   I   
B U E L     Z W R   R I     N   C H I O     D
A S L B   A P A C   N G   I G N   N   O     I
J U W T   F D T C I G S   Y O L   E   S B   N
  R I I   A   D E T       L E S F B J T B   G
  V L M   A   R E H       I W N C I I I L   K
  I I A       O W T A     D N U G P V E M   N
  V E T         S A P     L T G B A C   E   U
  E R A         Y         L   L R E         M
  D             L         L                 B
```

AUTOMATICALLY   GENERATE   PATHETIC   STINGY
BOUND   GNASHING   PEON   STUNT
CARP   HOSTILE   PUNCTUAL   SURVIVED
CONK   INCAPABLE   RABIES   THUGS
CONSCIENCE   INFECT   SANITATION   TOLERATE
CROUCHED   JABBERING   SCOWL   TORTURE
DAZZLE   JIVE   SENIORITY   TRAITOR
DISPOSITION   MATURE   SLEW   TRESPASSING
DROWSY   MUGS   SNITCH   ULTIMATE
DULL   MUMBLING   SOBBY   VITAL
EMULATE   NIBBLE   SQUARE   WAILING
EXECUTED   NUMB   STAGGERED   WELFARE
FROSTBITE   PACE   STILL   WILIER

Vocabulary Word Search 3 Watsons Go To Birmingham--1963

```
S H Y P N O T I Z E D G N I R E B B A J
U N C A C W F I N T I M I D A T E S G W
R N O T R Z E R X G Y B B S Z A D Q W D
V M N H O R D S O J E Y B X F M H U Q D
I T K E U C E T H S F N L E V I J A P S
V X S T C U T U S A T V E R B T K R W S
E J A I H R E N P H P B G R M L L E C D
D M T C E V R T X C N H I S A U S R Q B
D C Q G D E M V Q J S E A T T T A S N
I I F G M B I R W G H R C Z E R E F T Z
N Y S J F A N T I H V U W W A C K L I W
C V E P P L E K L D Q T R I A R L E N V
A B I D O L D X I G R R T K G I D W G J
P Y B B O S G S E N I O R I T Y L L Y J
A F A J G N I L R C R T W S N H Q I Y N
B J R U G I I T P J U N N S G F U L N X
L Q M Z D T S N I J C T Z T Y J E G X G
E S T N S C K L W O C S E J S Z C C S M
M J U O Q H L C R N N P X D L D F V T Q
Z O H J M U W Y B Q Y M N Y E D I Z M J
B H W D D L C M H V Q O X T W T N T B G
C A R P E M U L A T E L Z Z A D P A C E
L A U T C N U P T P R T O L E R A T E H
```

A large number (4)
A style that straightens curly hair (4)
Aid in the form of money and other benefits (7)
Amaze (6)
Angry expression (5)
Breed of large fish, including goldfish (4)
Create a feeling of fear in someone (10)
Crying (7)
Damage to limbs caused by freezing (9)
Disease of warm-blooded animals (6)
Distractions (10)
Faces (4)
Firm; strong-minded (10)
Full of hatred or anger (7)
Full of tears; crying (5)
Gangsters; violent criminals (5)
Give a disease to (6)
Grown-up; adult (6)
Having greater age or higher rank (9)
Having no motion (5)
Highest quality (8)
In a posture low to the ground (8)
Jazz or swing music (4)
More clever or deceiving (6)
Not able to do something (9)

Not able to feel emotions (4)
Not generous; not willing to share (6)
Not interesting; not exciting (4)
Obligated or certain to do something (5)
On time (8)
One who does something disloyal (7)
Out of touch; old fashioned (6)
Produce or make (8)
Put into a trance or sleep-like condition (10)
Put to death (8)
Put up with (8)
Randomly; not planned (11)
Related to mood or temperament (11)
Sad; causing feelings of pity (8)
Sleepy; tired (6)
Someone who tells on others (6)
Speed (4)
Stayed alive (8)
Stop; restrict (5)
Take small, quick, playful bites (6)
Talking very quickly (9)
To give pain or make another suffer (7)
Try to be like someone else (7)
Very important (5)
Very low-paid worker (4)

Vocabulary Word Search 3 Answer Key Watsons Go To Birmingham--1963

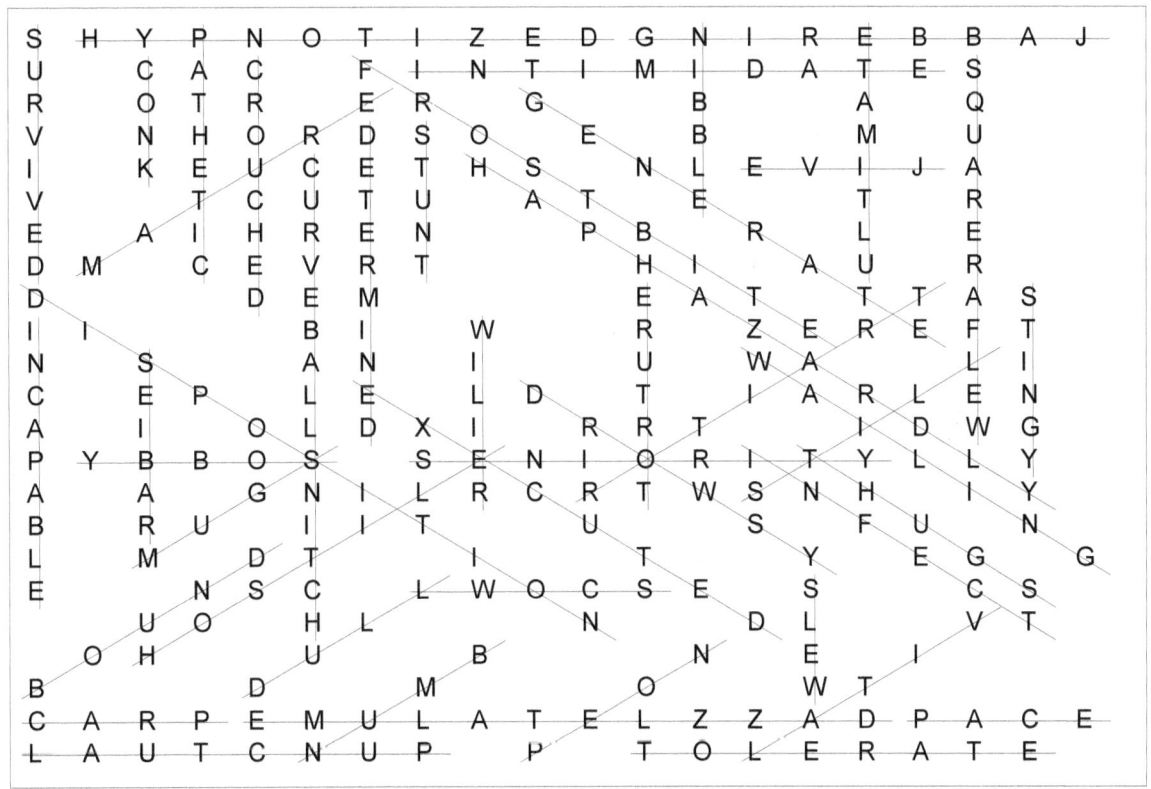

A large number (4)
A style that straightens curly hair (4)
Aid in the form of money and other benefits (7)
Amaze (6)
Angry expression (5)
Breed of large fish, including goldfish (4)
Create a feeling of fear in someone (10)
Crying (7)
Damage to limbs caused by freezing (9)
Disease of warm-blooded animals (6)
Distractions (10)
Faces (4)
Firm; strong-minded (10)
Full of hatred or anger (7)
Full of tears; crying (5)
Gangsters; violent criminals (5)
Give a disease to (6)
Grown-up; adult (6)
Having greater age or higher rank (9)
Having no motion (5)
Highest quality (8)
In a posture low to the ground (8)
Jazz or swing music (4)
More clever or deceiving (6)
Not able to do something (9)

Not able to feel emotions (4)
Not generous; not willing to share (6)
Not interesting; not exciting (4)
Obligated or certain to do something (5)
On time (8)
One who does something disloyal (7)
Out of touch; old fashioned (6)
Produce or make (8)
Put into a trance or sleep-like condition (10)
Put to death (8)
Put up with (8)
Randomly; not planned (11)
Related to mood or temperament (11)
Sad; causing feelings of pity (8)
Sleepy; tired (6)
Someone who tells on others (6)
Speed (4)
Stayed alive (8)
Stop; restrict (5)
Take small, quick, playful bites (6)
Talking very quickly (9)
To give pain or make another suffer (7)
Try to be like someone else (7)
Very important (5)
Very low-paid worker (4)

Vocabulary Word Search 4 Watsons Go To Birmingham--1963

```
I S O B B Y L D R A Z A H P A H D S S R
N B R T N W B M G E N E R A T E E Q N D
C Z Z N L K O N A W N L D K V I S U I X
A E T V S Z U Q Y T C D A I B E T A T W
P T C A R P N Y S W H U V A M M I R C R
A A P F R Q D Q W H T R R W Q U N E H Q
B D E H C U O R C O U L E B M L G P F L
L I D A Z Z L E M S P H P F D A Y Y S C
E M Y R R Q T A T V E O W P G T W L G K
M I B O K Z T J K S T S M A H E L R H Z
K T T T S I C P M C A T C T G A K D L Q
S N W I C E O G J O M I P H B M E D O Z
V I T A L K N O C W I L I E R U T R O T
Z L L R I I S I B L T E V T O W I O P Z
N L D T L L C N O K L R W I S N B W L R
Y S V B P E I E V R U Y T C T J T S R H
L G M R C R E N X C I C Y H A I S Y I D
W U H A R A N N G E E T U R G V O S H K
M M P X Y F C L I F C G Y M G E R T W D
S T I L L L E Y N B S U S F E B F U T J
W F W W L E R I U R B S T L R L Y N C J
N H Z U C W F B M V X L W E E K L T T B
G L D G N I R E B B A J E B D W L F N P
```

A large number (4)
A spiraling current of water (9)
A style that straightens curly hair (4)
Aid in the form of money and other benefits (7)
Amaze (6)
Angry expression (5)
Breed of large fish, including goldfish (4)
Create a feeling of fear in someone (10)
Crying (7)
Damage to limbs caused by freezing (9)
Disease of warm-blooded animals (6)
Distractions (10)
Done without thought (13)
Faces (4)
Full of hatred or anger (7)
Full of tears; crying (5)
Gangsters; violent criminals (5)
Give a disease to (6)
Grown-up; adult (6)
Having greater age or higher rank (9)
Having no motion (5)
Highest quality (8)
In a posture low to the ground (8)
Jazz or swing music (4)
More clever or deceiving (6)

Not able to do something (9)
Not able to feel emotions (4)
Not generous; not willing to share (6)
Not interesting; not exciting (4)
Obligated or certain to do something (5)
One who does something disloyal (7)
Out of touch; old fashioned (6)
Produce or make (8)
Put to death (8)
Randomly; not planned (11)
Sad; causing feelings of pity (8)
Sense of right and wrong (10)
Sleepy; tired (6)
Someone who tells on others (6)
Speaking unclearly in a low voice (8)
Speed (4)
Stayed alive (8)
Stop; restrict (5)
Take small, quick, playful bites (6)
Talking very quickly (9)
To give pain or make another suffer (7)
Try to be like someone else (7)
Very important (5)
Very low-paid worker (4)
Walked unsteadily (9)

Vocabulary Word Search 4 Answer Key Watsons Go To Birmingham--1963

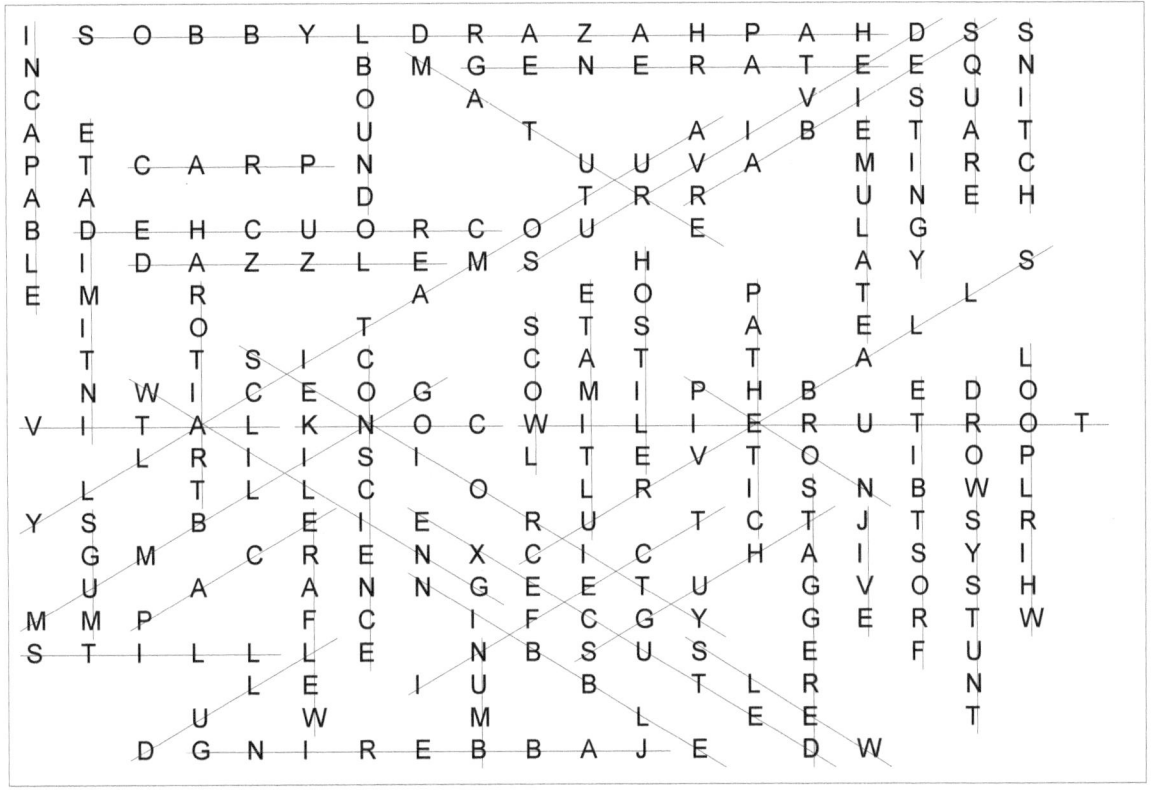

A large number (4)
A spiraling current of water (9)
A style that straightens curly hair (4)
Aid in the form of money and other benefits (7)
Amaze (6)
Angry expression (5)
Breed of large fish, including goldfish (4)
Create a feeling of fear in someone (10)
Crying (7)
Damage to limbs caused by freezing (9)
Disease of warm-blooded animals (6)
Distractions (10)
Done without thought (13)
Faces (4)
Full of hatred or anger (7)
Full of tears; crying (5)
Gangsters; violent criminals (5)
Give a disease to (6)
Grown-up; adult (6)
Having greater age or higher rank (9)
Having no motion (5)
Highest quality (8)
In a posture low to the ground (8)
Jazz or swing music (4)
More clever or deceiving (6)

Not able to do something (9)
Not able to feel emotions (4)
Not generous; not willing to share (6)
Not interesting; not exciting (4)
Obligated or certain to do something (5)
One who does something disloyal (7)
Out of touch; old fashioned (6)
Produce or make (8)
Put to death (8)
Randomly; not planned (11)
Sad; causing feelings of pity (8)
Sense of right and wrong (10)
Sleepy; tired (6)
Someone who tells on others (6)
Speaking unclearly in a low voice (8)
Speed (4)
Stayed alive (8)
Stop; restrict (5)
Take small, quick, playful bites (6)
Talking very quickly (9)
To give pain or make another suffer (7)
Try to be like someone else (7)
Very important (5)
Very low-paid worker (4)
Walked unsteadily (9)

Vocabulary Crossword 1 Watsons Go To Birmingham--1963

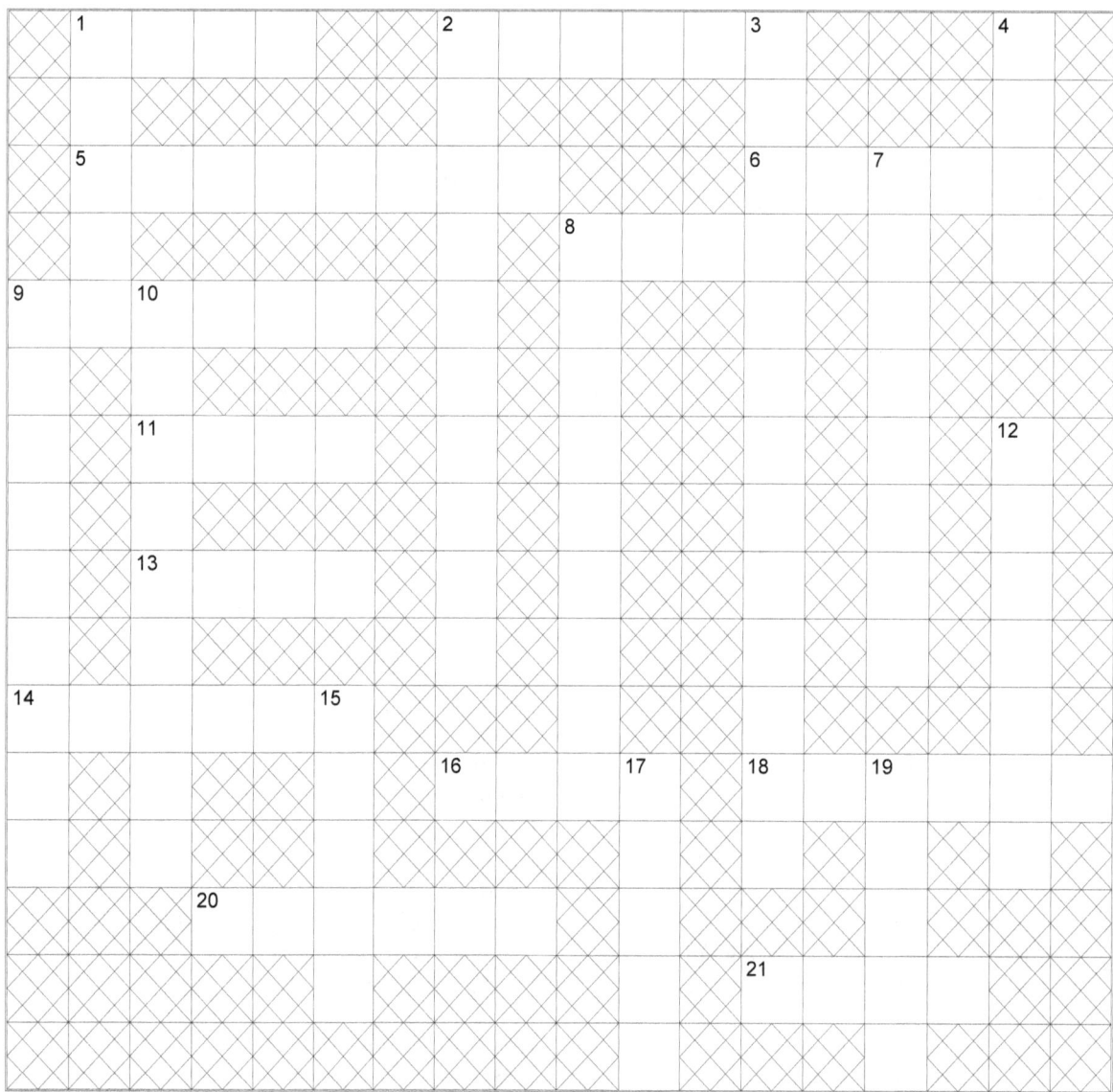

Across
1. A large number
2. Amaze
5. Highest quality
6. Very important
8. Jazz or swing music
9. Not generous; not willing to share
11. Breed of large fish, including goldfish
13. Very low-paid worker
14. Disease of warm-blooded animals
16. Faces
18. Take small, quick, playful bites
20. More clever or deceiving
21. A style that straightens curly hair

Down
1. Stop; restrict
2. Firm; strong-minded
3. Listening in when the speaker does not know it
4. Not interesting; not exciting
7. Put up with
8. Talking very quickly
9. Walked unsteadily
10. Not able to do something
12. Full of hatred or anger
15. Having no motion
17. Full of tears; crying
19. Obligated or certain to do something

Vocabulary Crossword 1 Watsons Go To Birmingham--1963

	1 S	L	E	W		2 D	A	Z	Z	L	3 E		4 D	
	T					E					A		U	
	5 U	L	T	I	M	A	T	E			6 V	I	7 T	A	L
	N					E		8 J	I	V	E		O		L
9 S	T	10 I	N	G	Y		R		A		S		L		
T		N					M		B		D		E		
A		11 C	A	R	P		I		B		R		R		12 H
G		A					N		E		O		A		O
G		13 P	E	O	N		E		R		P		T		S
E		A					D		I		P		E		T
14 R	A	B	I	15 E	S				N		I				I
E		L		T		16 M	U	17 G	S		18 N	I	19 B	B	L	E
D		E		I				O			G		O		E
			20 W	I	L	I	E	R			B		U		
				L				21 B			C	O	N	K	
								Y					D		

Across
1. A large number
2. Amaze
5. Highest quality
6. Very important
8. Jazz or swing music
9. Not generous; not willing to share
11. Breed of large fish, including goldfish
13. Very low-paid worker
14. Disease of warm-blooded animals
16. Faces
18. Take small, quick, playful bites
20. More clever or deceiving
21. A style that straightens curly hair

Down
1. Stop; restrict
2. Firm; strong-minded
3. Listening in when the speaker does not know it
4. Not interesting; not exciting
7. Put up with
8. Talking very quickly
9. Walked unsteadily
10. Not able to do something
12. Full of hatred or anger
15. Having no motion
17. Full of tears; crying
19. Obligated or certain to do something

Vocabulary Crossword 2 Watsons Go To Birmingham--1963

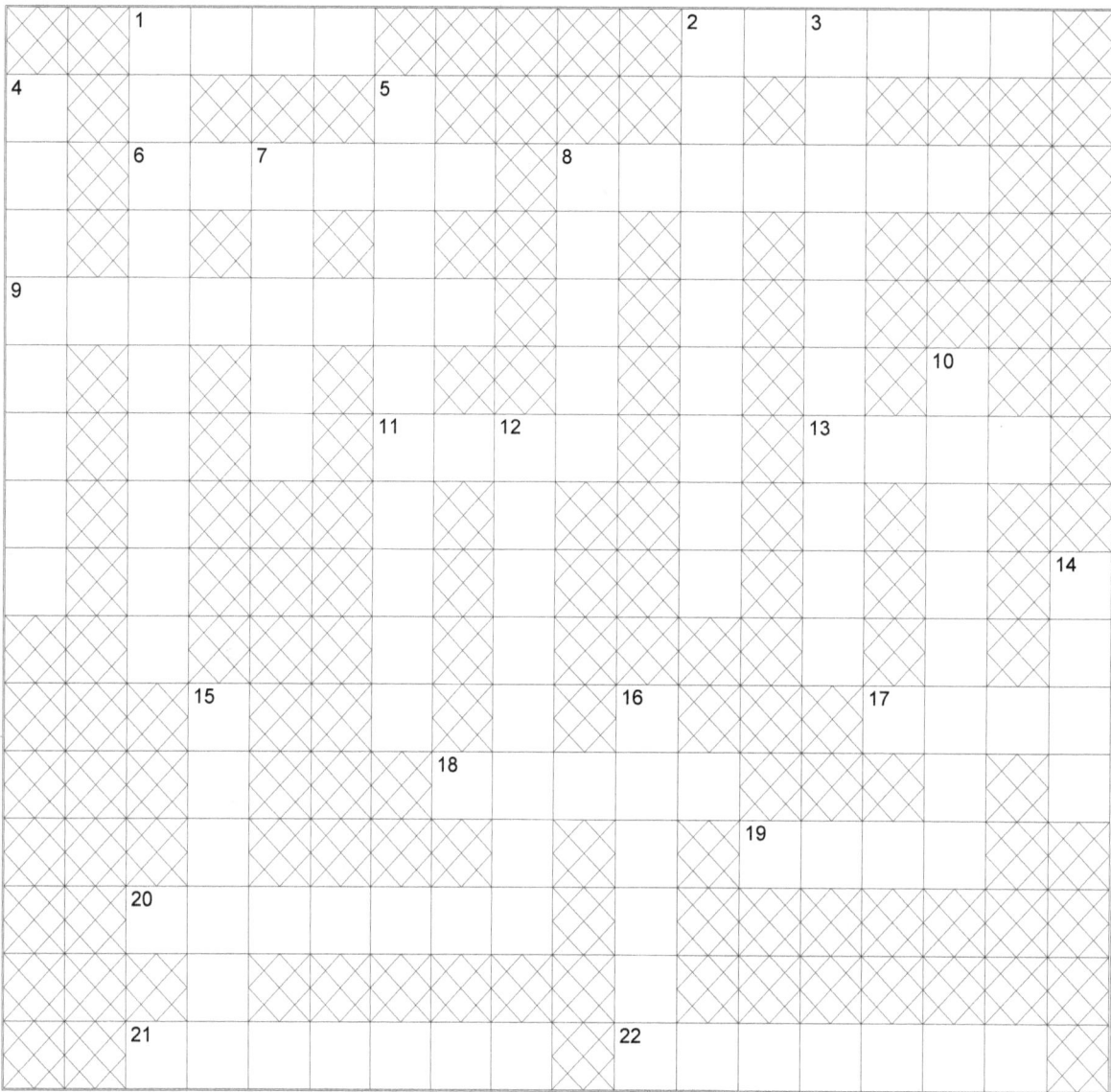

Across
1. Breed of large fish, including goldfish
2. Not generous; not willing to share
6. Disease of warm-blooded animals
8. One who does something disloyal
9. Put to death
11. Faces
13. Not interesting; not exciting
17. Speed
18. Very important
19. Jazz or swing music
20. Crying
21. Aid in the form of money and other benefits
22. Try to be like someone else

Down
1. Distractions
2. Walked unsteadily
3. Create a feeling of fear in someone
4. Put up with
5. Firm; strong-minded
7. Obligated or certain to do something
8. Gangsters; violent criminals
10. Highest quality
12. Clenching; grinding
14. A large number
15. Out of touch; old fashioned
16. Amaze

Vocabulary Crossword 2 Answer Key Watsons Go To Birmingham--1963

	¹C	A	R	P				²S	³T	I	N	G	Y	
⁴T	U			⁵D				T		N				
O	⁶R	A	⁷B	I	E	S		⁸T	R	A	I	T	O	R
L	V		O		T			H		G		I		
⁹E	X	E	C	U	T	E	D		U		G		M	
R	B		N		R				G		E		¹⁰U	
A	A		D		¹¹M	¹²U	G	S		R		¹³D	U	L	L
T	L				I		N			E		A		T	
E	L				N		A			D		T		I	¹⁴S
	S				E		S					E		M	L
		¹⁵S			D		H		¹⁶D				¹⁷P	A	C	E
		Q				¹⁸V	I	T	A	L				T		W
		U					N		Z			¹⁹J	I	V	E	
		²⁰W	A	I	L	I	N	G		Z						
		R								L						
		²¹W	E	L	F	A	R	E		²²E	M	U	L	A	T	E

Across
1. Breed of large fish, including goldfish
2. Not generous; not willing to share
6. Disease of warm-blooded animals
8. One who does something disloyal
9. Put to death
11. Faces
13. Not interesting; not exciting
17. Speed
18. Very important
19. Jazz or swing music
20. Crying
21. Aid in the form of money and other benefits
22. Try to be like someone else

Down
1. Distractions
2. Walked unsteadily
3. Create a feeling of fear in someone
4. Put up with
5. Firm; strong-minded
7. Obligated or certain to do something
8. Gangsters; violent criminals
10. Highest quality
12. Clenching; grinding
14. A large number
15. Out of touch; old fashioned
16. Amaze

Vocabulary Crossword 3 Watsons Go To Birmingham--1963

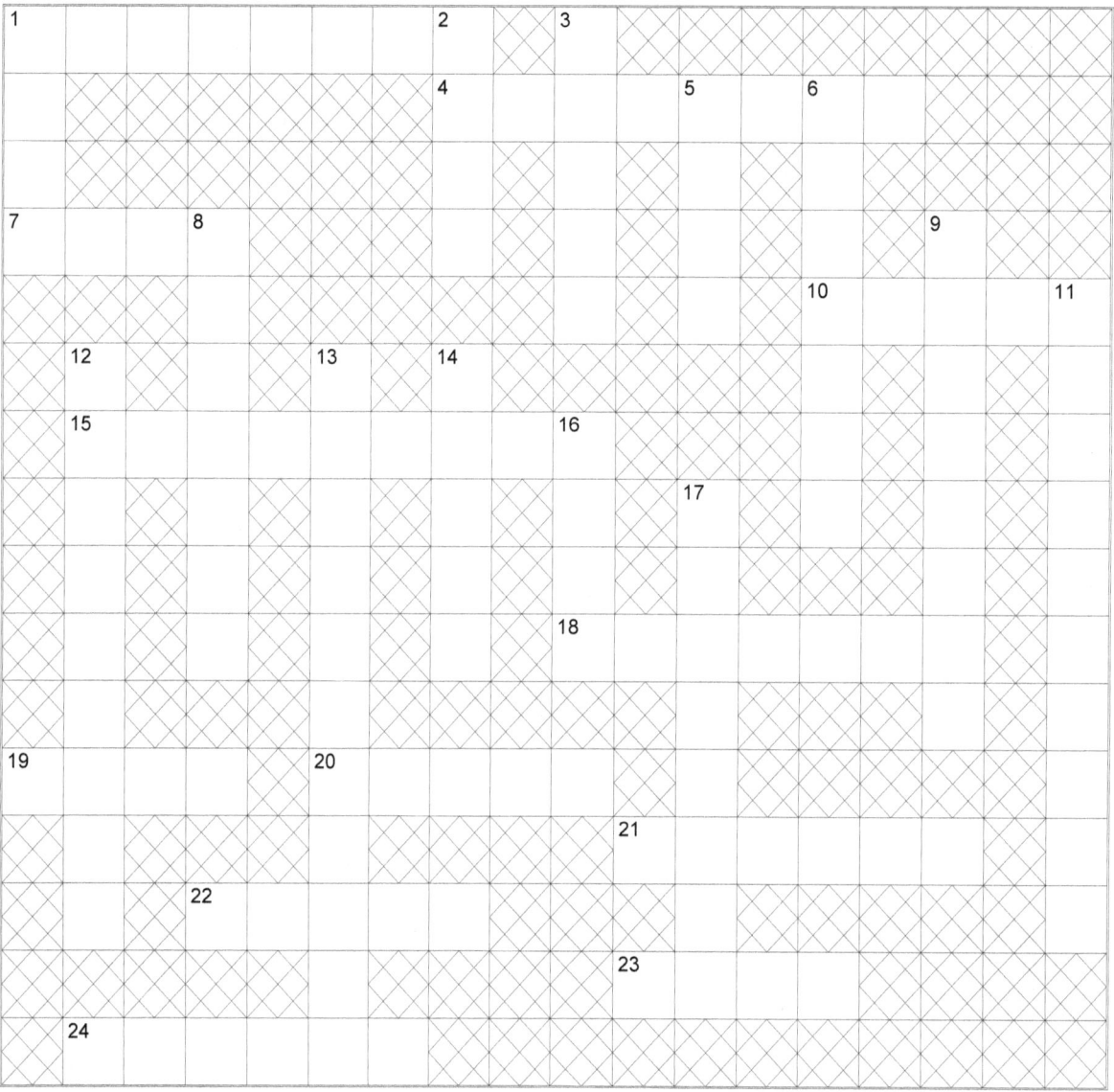

Across
1. In a posture low to the ground
4. Highest quality
7. Speed
10. Gangsters; violent criminals
15. Very funny
18. Aid in the form of money and other benefits
19. A style that straightens curly hair
20. Full of tears; crying
21. Amaze
22. Having no motion
23. Very low-paid worker
24. Not generous; not willing to share

Down
1. Breed of large fish, including goldfish
2. Not interesting; not exciting
3. Stop; restrict
5. Faces
6. To give pain or make another suffer
8. Try to be like someone else
9. Stayed alive
11. Related to health and cleanliness
12. A spiraling current of water
13. Going to a place without permission
14. Obligated or certain to do something
16. A large number
17. Put up with

Vocabulary Crossword 3 Answer Key Watsons Go To Birmingham--1963

1 C	R	O	U	C	H	E	2 D		3 S								
A							4 U	L	T	I	5 M	A	6 T	E			
R							L		U		U		O				
7 P	A	C	8 E				L		N		G		R		9 S		
			M						T		S		10 T	H	U	G	11 S
	12 W		U		13 T		14 B						U		R		A
	15 H	I	L	A	R	I	O	U	16 S				R		V		N
	I		A		E		U		L		17 T		E		I		I
	R		T		S		N		E		O				V		T
	L		E		P		D		18 W	E	L	F	A	R	E		A
	P				A						E				D		T
19 C	O	N	K		20 S	O	B	B	Y		R						I
	O				S					21 D	A	Z	Z	L	E		O
	L		22 S	T	I	L	L				T						N
					N					23 P	E	O	N				
	24 S	T	I	N	G	Y											

Across
1. In a posture low to the ground
4. Highest quality
7. Speed
10. Gangsters; violent criminals
15. Very funny
18. Aid in the form of money and other benefits
19. A style that straightens curly hair
20. Full of tears; crying
21. Amaze
22. Having no motion
23. Very low-paid worker
24. Not generous; not willing to share

.

Down
1. Breed of large fish, including goldfish
2. Not interesting; not exciting
3. Stop; restrict
5. Faces
6. To give pain or make another suffer
8. Try to be like someone else
9. Stayed alive
11. Related to health and cleanliness
12. A spiraling current of water
13. Going to a place without permission
14. Obligated or certain to do something
16. A large number
17. Put up with

Vocabulary Crossword 4 Watsons Go To Birmingham--1963

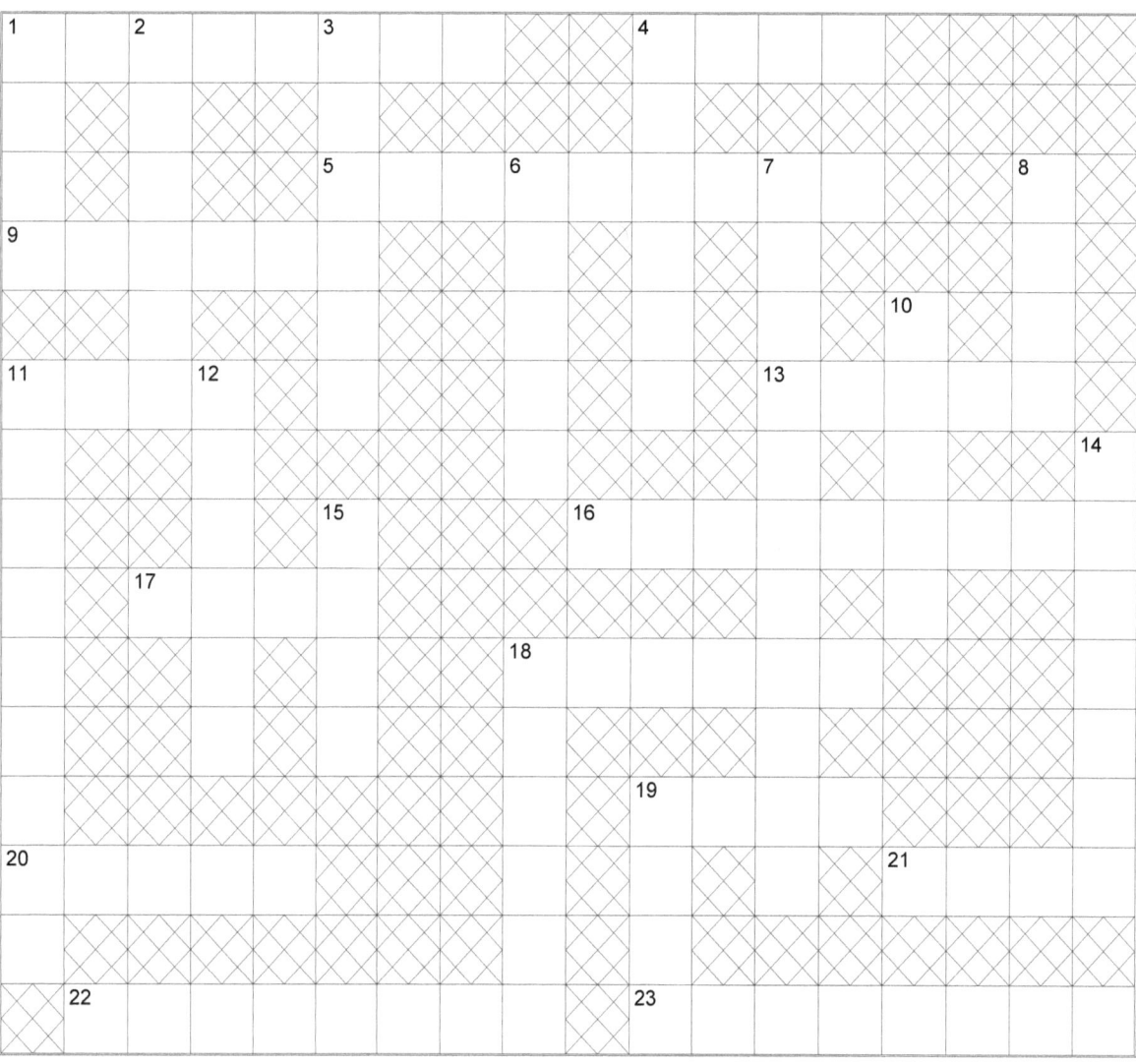

Across
1. Speaking unclearly in a low voice
4. Not able to feel emotions
5. Damage to limbs caused by freezing
9. Out of touch; old fashioned
11. A large number
13. Having no motion
16. Not able to do something
17. Jazz or swing music
18. Sleepy; tired
19. A style that straightens curly hair
20. Gangsters; violent criminals
21. Speed
22. Highest quality
23. Sad; causing feelings of pity

Down
1. Faces
2. Grown-up; adult
3. Give a disease to
4. Take small, quick, playful bites
6. Full of tears; crying
7. Going to a place without permission
8. Not interesting; not exciting
10. Very important
11. Having greater age or higher rank
12. More clever or deceiving
14. Aid in the form of money and other benefits
15. Very low-paid worker
18. Amaze
19. Breed of large fish, including goldfish

Vocabulary Crossword 4 Answer Key Watsons Go To Birmingham--1963

	1 M	2 U	M	B	L	3 I	N	G		4 N	U	M	B		
	U		A			N				I					
	G		T		5 F	R	O	6 S	T	B	I	7 T	E		8 D
	9 S	Q	U	A	R	E		O		B		R			U
			R		C			B		L		E		10 V	L
	11 S	L	12 E	W		T		B		E		13 S	T	I	L	L
	E		I					Y				P		T		14 W
	N		L		15 P		16 I	N	C	A	P	A	B	L	E
	I		17 J	I	V	E						S		L		L
	O		E		O			18 D	R	O	W	S	Y			F
	R		R		N			A				I				A
	I							Z		19 C	O	N	K			R
20 T	H	U	G	S				Z		A		G		21 P	A	C	E
Y								L		R						
	22 U	L	T	I	M	A	T	E		23 P	A	T	H	E	T	I	C

Across
1. Speaking unclearly in a low voice
4. Not able to feel emotions
5. Damage to limbs caused by freezing
9. Out of touch; old fashioned
11. A large number
13. Having no motion
16. Not able to do something
17. Jazz or swing music
18. Sleepy; tired
19. A style that straightens curly hair
20. Gangsters; violent criminals
21. Speed
22. Highest quality
23. Sad; causing feelings of pity

Down
1. Faces
2. Grown-up; adult
3. Give a disease to
4. Take small, quick, playful bites
6. Full of tears; crying
7. Going to a place without permission
8. Not interesting; not exciting
10. Very important
11. Having greater age or higher rank
12. More clever or deceiving
14. Aid in the form of money and other benefits
15. Very low-paid worker
18. Amaze
19. Breed of large fish, including goldfish

Vocabulary Juggle Letters 1 Watsons Go To Birmingham--1963

1. HTCISN = 1. _____
   Someone who tells on others

2. KOCN = 2. _____
   A style that straightens curly hair

3. LIAVT = 3. _____
   Very important

4. ANPIRSSGETS = 4. _____
   Going to a place without permission

5. BBSOY = 5. _____
   Full of tears; crying

6. RIEYSITON = 6. _____
   Having greater age or higher rank

7. ZDYHPRAALAH = 7. _____
   Randomly; not planned

8. UGSTH = 8. _____
   Gangsters; violent criminals

9. BLAANPICE = 9. _____
   Not able to do something

10. GSNTYI =10. _____
    Not generous; not willing to share

11. LAULMAYACOTTI =11. _____
    Done without thought

12. LULD =12. _____
    Not interesting; not exciting

13. ENDETRDEIM =13. _____
    Firm; strong-minded

14. DBNOU =14. _____
    Obligated or certain to do something

15. CUTPNULA =15. _____
    On time

16. OSCIENECCN =16. _____
    Sense of right and wrong

Vocabulary Juggle Letters 1 Answer Key Watsons Go To Birmingham--1963

1. HTCISN = 1. SNITCH
   Someone who tells on others
2. KOCN = 2. CONK
   A style that straightens curly hair
3. LIAVT = 3. VITAL
   Very important
4. ANPIRSSGETS = 4. TRESPASSING
   Going to a place without permission
5. BBSOY = 5. SOBBY
   Full of tears; crying
6. RIEYSITON = 6. SENIORITY
   Having greater age or higher rank
7. ZDYHPRAALAH = 7. HAPHAZARDLY
   Randomly; not planned
8. UGSTH = 8. THUGS
   Gangsters; violent criminals
9. BLAANPICE = 9. INCAPABLE
   Not able to do something
10. GSNTYI = 10. STINGY
    Not generous; not willing to share
11. LAULMAYACOTTI = 11. AUTOMATICALLY
    Done without thought
12. LULD = 12. DULL
    Not interesting; not exciting
13. ENDETRDEIM = 13. DETERMINED
    Firm; strong-minded
14. DBNOU = 14. BOUND
    Obligated or certain to do something
15. CUTPNULA = 15. PUNCTUAL
    On time
16. OSCIENECCN = 16. CONSCIENCE
    Sense of right and wrong

Vocabulary Juggle Letters 2 Watsons Go To Birmingham--1963

1. INSATOITNA = 1. _____
   Related to health and cleanliness

2. RSDVUEIV = 2. _____
   Stayed alive

3. TILLS = 3. _____
   Having no motion

4. NFTECI = 4. _____
   Give a disease to

5. ROTBFITES = 5. _____
   Damage to limbs caused by freezing

6. SWLCO = 6. _____
   Angry expression

7. LPIACEBAN = 7. _____
   Not able to do something

8. TNSHCI = 8. _____
   Someone who tells on others

9. RTTEOUR = 9. _____
   To give pain or make another suffer

10. EPON = 10. _____
    Very low-paid worker

11. WLES = 11. _____
    A large number

12. YTSNGI = 12. _____
    Not generous; not willing to share

13. SMUG = 13. _____
    Faces

14. OBYBS = 14. _____
    Full of tears; crying

15. LLDU = 15. _____
    Not interesting; not exciting

16. AHTECITP = 16. _____
    Sad; causing feelings of pity

Vocabulary Juggle Letters 2 Answer Key Watsons Go To Birmingham--1963

1. INSATOITNA = 1. SANITATION
Related to health and cleanliness

2. RSDVUEIV = 2. SURVIVED
Stayed alive

3. TILLS = 3. STILL
Having no motion

4. NFTECI = 4. INFECT
Give a disease to

5. ROTBFITES = 5. FROSTBITE
Damage to limbs caused by freezing

6. SWLCO = 6. SCOWL
Angry expression

7. LPIACEBAN = 7. INCAPABLE
Not able to do something

8. TNSHCI = 8. SNITCH
Someone who tells on others

9. RTTEOUR = 9. TORTURE
To give pain or make another suffer

10. EPON = 10. PEON
Very low-paid worker

11. WLES = 11. SLEW
A large number

12. YTSNGI = 12. STINGY
Not generous; not willing to share

13. SMUG = 13. MUGS
Faces

14. OBYBS = 14. SOBBY
Full of tears; crying

15. LLDU = 15. DULL
Not interesting; not exciting

16. AHTECITP = 16. PATHETIC
Sad; causing feelings of pity

Copyrighted

Vocabulary Juggle Letters 3 Watsons Go To Birmingham--1963

1. WSLOC = 1. _____
   Angry expression

2. IEBBNL = 2. _____
   Take small, quick, playful bites

3. TACUPNLU = 3. _____
   On time

4. IILEWR = 4. _____
   More clever or deceiving

5. YMAULTLAAITCO = 5. _____
   Done without thought

6. MBIMNLGU = 6. _____
   Speaking unclearly in a low voice

7. EEEGNART = 7. _____
   Produce or make

8. GAGNHSIN = 8. _____
   Clenching; grinding

9. SLAECVLURB = 9. _____
   Distractions

10. ILOLWPOHR =10. _____
    A spiraling current of water

11. MTEELUA =11. _____
    Try to be like someone else

12. LDLU =12. _____
    Not interesting; not exciting

13. ECCOECSNIN =13. _____
    Sense of right and wrong

14. BOSBY =14. _____
    Full of tears; crying

15. ATASINNOTI =15. _____
    Related to health and cleanliness

16. TEURORT =16. _____
    To give pain or make another suffer

Vocabulary Juggle Letters 3 Answer Key Watsons Go To Birmingham--1963

1. WSLOC = 1. SCOWL
   Angry expression

2. IEBBNL = 2. NIBBLE
   Take small, quick, playful bites

3. TACUPNLU = 3. PUNCTUAL
   On time

4. IILEWR = 4. WILIER
   More clever or deceiving

5. YMAULTLAAITCO = 5. AUTOMATICALLY
   Done without thought

6. MBIMNLGU = 6. MUMBLING
   Speaking unclearly in a low voice

7. EEEGNART = 7. GENERATE
   Produce or make

8. GAGNHSIN = 8. GNASHING
   Clenching; grinding

9. SLAECVLURB = 9. CURVEBALLS
   Distractions

10. ILOLWPOHR =10. WHIRLPOOL
    A spiraling current of water

11. MTEELUA =11. EMULATE
    Try to be like someone else

12. LDLU =12. DULL
    Not interesting; not exciting

13. ECCOECSNIN =13. CONSCIENCE
    Sense of right and wrong

14. BOSBY =14. SOBBY
    Full of tears; crying

15. ATASINNOTI =15. SANITATION
    Related to health and cleanliness

16. TEURORT =16. TORTURE
    To give pain or make another suffer

Vocabulary Juggle Letters 4 Watsons Go To Birmingham--1963

1. DUOBN = 1. _____
Obligated or certain to do something

2. NNAISGGH = 2. _____
Clenching; grinding

3. ORLEATET = 3. _____
Put up with

4. ELFAWRE = 4. _____
Aid in the form of money and other benefits

5. NCBEIALAP = 5. _____
Not able to do something

6. RTSISAPNSGE = 6. _____
Going to a place without permission

7. CEHAPITT = 7. _____
Sad; causing feelings of pity

8. OOLWHRIPL = 8. _____
A spiraling current of water

9. TELTUECOCRED = 9. _____
Died by electric shock

10. TUAMER =10. _____
Grown-up; adult

11. TINSYG =11. _____
Not generous; not willing to share

12. GAESPVEDRINPO =12. _____
Listening in when the speaker does not know it

13. USIARLOHI =13. _____
Very funny

14. LUDL =14. _____
Not interesting; not exciting

15. SURAQE =15. _____
Out of touch; old fashioned

16. TNOREIYSI =16. _____
Having greater age or higher rank

Copyrighted

Vocabulary Juggle Letters 4 Answer Key Watsons Go To Birmingham--1963

1. DUOBN = 1. BOUND
   Obligated or certain to do something

2. NNAISGGH = 2. GNASHING
   Clenching; grinding

3. ORLEATET = 3. TOLERATE
   Put up with

4. ELFAWRE = 4. WELFARE
   Aid in the form of money and other benefits

5. NCBEIALAP = 5. INCAPABLE
   Not able to do something

6. RTSISAPNSGE = 6. TRESPASSING
   Going to a place without permission

7. CEHAPITT = 7. PATHETIC
   Sad; causing feelings of pity

8. OOLWHRIPL = 8. WHIRLPOOL
   A spiraling current of water

9. TELTUECOCRED = 9. ELECTROCUTED
   Died by electric shock

10. TUAMER =10. MATURE
    Grown-up; adult

11. TINSYG =11. STINGY
    Not generous; not willing to share

12. GAESPVEDRINPO =12. EAVESDROPPING
    Listening in when the speaker does not know it

13. USIARLOHI =13. HILARIOUS
    Very funny

14. LUDL =14. DULL
    Not interesting; not exciting

15. SURAQE =15. SQUARE
    Out of touch; old fashioned

16. TNOREIYSI =16. SENIORITY
    Having greater age or higher rank

AUTOMATICALLY	Done without thought
BOUND	Obligated or certain to do something
CARP	Breed of large fish, including goldfish
CONK	A style that straightens curly hair
CONSCIENCE	Sense of right and wrong

CROUCHED	In a posture low to the ground
CURVEBALLS	Distractions
DAZZLE	Amaze
DETERMINED	Firm; strong-minded
DISPOSITION	Related to mood or temperament

DROWSY	Sleepy; tired
DULL	Not interesting; not exciting
EAVESDROPPING	Listening in when the speaker does not know it
ELECTROCUTED	Died by electric shock
EMULATE	Try to be like someone else

EXECUTED	Put to death
FROSTBITE	Damage to limbs caused by freezing
GENERATE	Produce or make
GNASHING	Clenching; grinding
HAPHAZARDLY	Randomly; not planned

HILARIOUS	Very funny
HOSTILE	Full of hatred or anger
HYPNOTIZED	Put into a trance or sleep-like condition
INCAPABLE	Not able to do something
INFECT	Give a disease to

INTIMIDATE	Create a feeling of fear in someone
JABBERING	Talking very quickly
JIVE	Jazz or swing music
MATURE	Grown-up; adult
MUGS	Faces

MUMBLING	Speaking unclearly in a low voice
NIBBLE	Take small, quick, playful bites
NUMB	Not able to feel emotions
PACE	Speed
PATHETIC	Sad; causing feelings of pity

PEON	Very low-paid worker
PUNCTUAL	On time
RABIES	Disease of warm-blooded animals
SANITATION	Related to health and cleanliness
SCOWL	Angry expression

SENIORITY	Having greater age or higher rank
SLEW	A large number
SNITCH	Someone who tells on others
SOBBY	Full of tears; crying
SQUARE	Out of touch; old fashioned

STAGGERED	Walked unsteadily
STILL	Having no motion
STINGY	Not generous; not willing to share
STUNT	Stop; restrict
SURVIVED	Stayed alive

THUGS	Gangsters; violent criminals
TOLERATE	Put up with
TORTURE	To give pain or make another suffer
TRAITOR	One who does something disloyal
TRESPASSING	Going to a place without permission

ULTIMATE	Highest quality
VITAL	Very important
WAILING	Crying
WELFARE	Aid in the form of money and other benefits
WHIRLPOOL	A spiraling current of water

WILIER

More clever or deceiving

Watsons Go To Birmingham Vocabulary

CONSCIENCE	TOLERATE	MUGS	SOBBY	HYPNOTIZED
WILIER	SCOWL	BOUND	STUNT	MUMBLING
STINGY	SENIORITY	FREE SPACE	HAPHAZARDLY	HOSTILE
WAILING	GNASHING	TRESPASSING	STILL	NUMB
DISPOSITION	EXECUTED	SURVIVED	CONK	SQUARE

Watsons Go To Birmingham Vocabulary

PUNCTUAL	CARP	CURVEBALLS	JIVE	CROUCHED
DETERMINED	STAGGERED	HILARIOUS	SNITCH	SLEW
RABIES	DULL	FREE SPACE	INTIMIDATE	TORTURE
TRAITOR	FROSTBITE	DROWSY	ULTIMATE	INCAPABLE
GENERATE	WELFARE	ELECTROCUTED	PEON	JABBERING

Watsons Go To Birmingham Vocabulary

PUNCTUAL	MUMBLING	AUTOMATICALLY	BOUND	THUGS
NIBBLE	HAPHAZARDLY	TRESPASSING	INFECT	PATHETIC
WILIER	EXECUTED	FREE SPACE	GNASHING	ELECTROCUTED
ULTIMATE	SANITATION	NUMB	STILL	WHIRLPOOL
STAGGERED	GENERATE	CROUCHED	DISPOSITION	CURVEBALLS

Watsons Go To Birmingham Vocabulary

CONK	DAZZLE	HYPNOTIZED	SCOWL	STINGY
TORTURE	EMULATE	INCAPABLE	DROWSY	FROSTBITE
SLEW	PACE	FREE SPACE	HILARIOUS	HOSTILE
STUNT	CARP	JIVE	CONSCIENCE	DETERMINED
SURVIVED	SQUARE	MUGS	WELFARE	SOBBY

Watsons Go To Birmingham Vocabulary

CARP	PEON	MUMBLING	SENIORITY	WILIER
DAZZLE	SANITATION	ELECTROCUTED	SOBBY	MATURE
NUMB	SNITCH	FREE SPACE	HYPNOTIZED	DETERMINED
GNASHING	TOLERATE	FROSTBITE	HAPHAZARDLY	JABBERING
DISPOSITION	STILL	CONSCIENCE	ULTIMATE	EXECUTED

Watsons Go To Birmingham Vocabulary

NIBBLE	VITAL	SCOWL	TRAITOR	SURVIVED
THUGS	STAGGERED	DROWSY	CROUCHED	PUNCTUAL
GENERATE	EAVESDROPPING	FREE SPACE	SQUARE	WHIRLPOOL
INFECT	BOUND	PACE	HILARIOUS	TORTURE
STUNT	SLEW	JIVE	AUTOMATICALLY	MUGS

Watsons Go To Birmingham Vocabulary

CROUCHED	PACE	PUNCTUAL	WELFARE	SNITCH
STAGGERED	HAPHAZARDLY	TORTURE	AUTOMATICALLY	EXECUTED
NIBBLE	DETERMINED	FREE SPACE	HYPNOTIZED	WAILING
FROSTBITE	EAVESDROPPING	ELECTROCUTED	THUGS	CONSCIENCE
STUNT	MUGS	INCAPABLE	JIVE	DULL

Watsons Go To Birmingham Vocabulary

EMULATE	VITAL	INFECT	INTIMIDATE	GNASHING
CURVEBALLS	TRAITOR	GENERATE	SOBBY	WILIER
SURVIVED	SENIORITY	FREE SPACE	STILL	STINGY
HILARIOUS	JABBERING	PATHETIC	SLEW	SQUARE
MATURE	DROWSY	CONK	RABIES	HOSTILE

Watsons Go To Birmingham Vocabulary

DULL	PATHETIC	TOLERATE	HYPNOTIZED	DISPOSITION
GNASHING	CARP	NIBBLE	BOUND	INFECT
TRAITOR	ELECTROCUTED	FREE SPACE	SCOWL	CROUCHED
SANITATION	RABIES	EAVESDROPPING	PEON	SQUARE
INTIMIDATE	INCAPABLE	NUMB	THUGS	MUGS

Watsons Go To Birmingham Vocabulary

FROSTBITE	WILIER	HAPHAZARDLY	WELFARE	JIVE
MATURE	AUTOMATICALLY	GENERATE	STILL	SOBBY
VITAL	SENIORITY	FREE SPACE	TRESPASSING	TORTURE
DETERMINED	STINGY	SNITCH	WAILING	WHIRLPOOL
CONK	EXECUTED	EMULATE	CONSCIENCE	STAGGERED

Watsons Go To Birmingham Vocabulary

WILIER	HAPHAZARDLY	PEON	JIVE	SCOWL
WELFARE	ULTIMATE	SQUARE	TRESPASSING	CARP
EXECUTED	MUGS	FREE SPACE	WHIRLPOOL	EMULATE
SENIORITY	STAGGERED	HILARIOUS	NUMB	STILL
DETERMINED	INTIMIDATE	TOLERATE	INCAPABLE	DULL

Watsons Go To Birmingham Vocabulary

DISPOSITION	SANITATION	DAZZLE	INFECT	SOBBY
CROUCHED	PUNCTUAL	TORTURE	AUTOMATICALLY	BOUND
CONK	CONSCIENCE	FREE SPACE	HOSTILE	GENERATE
PACE	STINGY	WAILING	ELECTROCUTED	SURVIVED
CURVEBALLS	MATURE	MUMBLING	NIBBLE	SLEW

Watsons Go To Birmingham Vocabulary

CROUCHED	STUNT	DETERMINED	ELECTROCUTED	DISPOSITION
SURVIVED	INFECT	BOUND	GENERATE	SOBBY
GNASHING	CURVEBALLS	FREE SPACE	NIBBLE	SLEW
CARP	DROWSY	EAVESDROPPING	ULTIMATE	MUMBLING
PUNCTUAL	AUTOMATICALLY	HYPNOTIZED	VITAL	WAILING

Watsons Go To Birmingham Vocabulary

WILIER	HAPHAZARDLY	STAGGERED	DULL	EXECUTED
PEON	STILL	RABIES	STINGY	WELFARE
HILARIOUS	PATHETIC	FREE SPACE	PACE	SQUARE
HOSTILE	TRESPASSING	TRAITOR	NUMB	SENIORITY
INCAPABLE	SANITATION	SCOWL	INTIMIDATE	JABBERING

Watsons Go To Birmingham Vocabulary

STINGY	BOUND	SOBBY	TRAITOR	NIBBLE
PEON	SURVIVED	NUMB	SLEW	WAILING
GENERATE	HILARIOUS	FREE SPACE	TRESPASSING	MUMBLING
SNITCH	EMULATE	TOLERATE	GNASHING	VITAL
JIVE	CROUCHED	RABIES	DAZZLE	PATHETIC

Watsons Go To Birmingham Vocabulary

WELFARE	DULL	EAVESDROPPING	CURVEBALLS	FROSTBITE
DISPOSITION	STUNT	MUGS	DROWSY	INTIMIDATE
SQUARE	HAPHAZARDLY	FREE SPACE	HYPNOTIZED	AUTOMATICALLY
ELECTROCUTED	STAGGERED	PACE	HOSTILE	SENIORITY
DETERMINED	EXECUTED	PUNCTUAL	THUGS	CONK

Watsons Go To Birmingham Vocabulary

MUMBLING	BOUND	CROUCHED	GENERATE	STINGY
TORTURE	VITAL	DETERMINED	STUNT	EMULATE
EXECUTED	STAGGERED	FREE SPACE	DROWSY	SCOWL
SANITATION	PACE	TOLERATE	NUMB	WHIRLPOOL
THUGS	JIVE	CONK	INCAPABLE	ULTIMATE

Watsons Go To Birmingham Vocabulary

CONSCIENCE	JABBERING	MUGS	HILARIOUS	HAPHAZARDLY
INFECT	RABIES	ELECTROCUTED	WAILING	TRESPASSING
HYPNOTIZED	WELFARE	FREE SPACE	DAZZLE	SOBBY
PEON	SQUARE	INTIMIDATE	SLEW	MATURE
DULL	GNASHING	EAVESDROPPING	CARP	NIBBLE

Watsons Go To Birmingham Vocabulary

MATURE	HYPNOTIZED	SENIORITY	WILIER	PEON
HAPHAZARDLY	CARP	INTIMIDATE	HOSTILE	BOUND
SNITCH	HILARIOUS	FREE SPACE	STILL	WELFARE
SOBBY	PACE	CURVEBALLS	ULTIMATE	DROWSY
DISPOSITION	THUGS	JIVE	DULL	DAZZLE

Watsons Go To Birmingham Vocabulary

TORTURE	SLEW	STUNT	TRESPASSING	AUTOMATICALLY
ELECTROCUTED	NUMB	CONK	MUMBLING	VITAL
INCAPABLE	DETERMINED	FREE SPACE	GENERATE	SANITATION
STINGY	TOLERATE	PATHETIC	SURVIVED	WAILING
TRAITOR	CROUCHED	EAVESDROPPING	CONSCIENCE	MUGS

Watsons Go To Birmingham Vocabulary

WHIRLPOOL	SOBBY	DISPOSITION	FROSTBITE	STINGY
VITAL	CURVEBALLS	MUMBLING	BOUND	TRAITOR
MATURE	DROWSY	FREE SPACE	MUGS	SURVIVED
DAZZLE	SLEW	THUGS	NIBBLE	CROUCHED
AUTOMATICALLY	DETERMINED	WELFARE	HOSTILE	SENIORITY

Watsons Go To Birmingham Vocabulary

INTIMIDATE	INFECT	WILIER	TRESPASSING	TORTURE
PACE	INCAPABLE	GENERATE	PEON	HYPNOTIZED
JIVE	RABIES	FREE SPACE	ELECTROCUTED	CARP
STUNT	TOLERATE	HAPHAZARDLY	SANITATION	SNITCH
CONSCIENCE	CONK	DULL	WAILING	SCOWL

Watsons Go To Birmingham Vocabulary

CONSCIENCE	EXECUTED	INFECT	SURVIVED	WAILING
PEON	CONK	ULTIMATE	STILL	WHIRLPOOL
EMULATE	DULL	FREE SPACE	TORTURE	CARP
DISPOSITION	PUNCTUAL	RABIES	BOUND	GENERATE
SLEW	HYPNOTIZED	PACE	STAGGERED	STUNT

Watsons Go To Birmingham Vocabulary

MUGS	THUGS	HOSTILE	FROSTBITE	DROWSY
SQUARE	CURVEBALLS	MUMBLING	NIBBLE	INTIMIDATE
TOLERATE	VITAL	FREE SPACE	SENIORITY	SOBBY
SANITATION	SNITCH	DETERMINED	NUMB	CROUCHED
WILIER	JIVE	WELFARE	SCOWL	AUTOMATICALLY

Watsons Go To Birmingham Vocabulary

TRAITOR	DULL	INCAPABLE	DISPOSITION	STILL
JIVE	AUTOMATICALLY	TORTURE	ULTIMATE	WILIER
WELFARE	RABIES	FREE SPACE	SURVIVED	GNASHING
CARP	SNITCH	MATURE	EXECUTED	INFECT
BOUND	NUMB	TOLERATE	MUGS	DETERMINED

Watsons Go To Birmingham Vocabulary

ELECTROCUTED	GENERATE	SOBBY	CONSCIENCE	HILARIOUS
HAPHAZARDLY	CONK	HYPNOTIZED	THUGS	WHIRLPOOL
NIBBLE	DROWSY	FREE SPACE	JABBERING	HOSTILE
EAVESDROPPING	PATHETIC	SQUARE	PEON	CROUCHED
MUMBLING	PACE	WAILING	SCOWL	EMULATE

Watsons Go To Birmingham Vocabulary

NIBBLE	TORTURE	ULTIMATE	TRAITOR	CONK
CONSCIENCE	SENIORITY	STAGGERED	WELFARE	JIVE
DROWSY	DULL	FREE SPACE	EMULATE	WILIER
SCOWL	AUTOMATICALLY	FROSTBITE	INCAPABLE	EXECUTED
PEON	HAPHAZARDLY	MATURE	BOUND	GNASHING

Watsons Go To Birmingham Vocabulary

PACE	PUNCTUAL	SLEW	SOBBY	JABBERING
ELECTROCUTED	EAVESDROPPING	PATHETIC	SQUARE	DETERMINED
THUGS	STILL	FREE SPACE	HILARIOUS	GENERATE
INTIMIDATE	HOSTILE	SNITCH	TRESPASSING	WAILING
CROUCHED	CARP	DISPOSITION	TOLERATE	MUMBLING

Watsons Go To Birmingham Vocabulary

GENERATE	INCAPABLE	TORTURE	INFECT	DROWSY
SLEW	JABBERING	SOBBY	AUTOMATICALLY	PEON
CURVEBALLS	CROUCHED	FREE SPACE	JIVE	INTIMIDATE
MUGS	SQUARE	HYPNOTIZED	PACE	WHIRLPOOL
HAPHAZARDLY	EAVESDROPPING	HILARIOUS	STUNT	HOSTILE

Watsons Go To Birmingham Vocabulary

MUMBLING	STINGY	PATHETIC	SNITCH	CONSCIENCE
SCOWL	MATURE	DETERMINED	WILIER	WAILING
CARP	PUNCTUAL	FREE SPACE	TOLERATE	DULL
ULTIMATE	NIBBLE	CONK	DAZZLE	SENIORITY
SURVIVED	TRESPASSING	STILL	NUMB	BOUND

Watsons Go To Birmingham Vocabulary

CONSCIENCE	PUNCTUAL	STINGY	EAVESDROPPING	INTIMIDATE
STILL	INCAPABLE	AUTOMATICALLY	EMULATE	ELECTROCUTED
VITAL	DISPOSITION	FREE SPACE	JIVE	SOBBY
HOSTILE	GNASHING	TRAITOR	RABIES	CONK
SNITCH	DAZZLE	WHIRLPOOL	TRESPASSING	PACE

Watsons Go To Birmingham Vocabulary

CURVEBALLS	SENIORITY	SLEW	DULL	HYPNOTIZED
GENERATE	NIBBLE	JABBERING	HAPHAZARDLY	CROUCHED
TORTURE	THUGS	FREE SPACE	ULTIMATE	NUMB
SQUARE	FROSTBITE	DETERMINED	STAGGERED	SURVIVED
INFECT	MUGS	PATHETIC	TOLERATE	WELFARE